MY WAY OR THE
HIGHWAY

HARRY E. CHAMBERS

MY WAY OR THE HIGHWAY

THE MICROMANAGEMENT SURVIVAL GUIDE

BERRETT-KOEHLER PUBLISHERS, INC.
San Francisco

Berrett-Koehler Publishers, Inc.
235 Montgomery Street, Suite 650
San Francisco, CA 94104-2916
Tel: (415) 288-0260   Fax: (415) 362-2512   www.bkconnection.com

ORDERING INFORMATION

Quantity sales. Special discounts are available on quantity purchases by corporations, associations, and others. For details, contact the "Special Sales Department" at the Berrett-Koehler address above.

Individual sales. Berrett-Koehler publications are available through most bookstores. They can also be ordered direct from Berrett-Koehler: Tel: (800) 929-2929; Fax: (802) 864-7626; www.bkconnection.com

Orders for college textbook/course adoption use. Please contact Berrett-Koehler: Tel: (800) 929-2929; Fax: (802) 864-7626.

Orders by U.S. trade bookstores and wholesalers. Please contact Publishers Group West, 1700 Fourth Street, Berkeley, CA 94710. Tel: (510) 528-1444; Fax (510) 528-3444.

Production Management: Michael Bass Associates

Berrett-Koehler and the BK logo are registered trademarks of Berrett-Koehler Publishers, Inc.

Printed in the United States of America

Berrett-Koehler books are printed on long-lasting acid-free paper. When it is available, we choose paper that has been manufactured by environmentally responsible processes. These may include using trees grown in sustainable forests, incorporating recycled paper, minimizing chlorine in bleaching, or recycling the energy produced at the paper mill.

Library of Congress Cataloging-in-Publication Data
Chambers, Harry (Harry E.)
    My way or the highway: the micromanagement survival guide / by Harry E. Chambers.
      p.   cm
    Includes index.
    ISBN 1-57675-296-8
      1. Communication in management. 2. Supervision of employees.
    3. Interpersonal communication. 4. Industrial relations. I. Title.
    HD30.3.C453 2004
    658.4—dc22
                                                                2004050707

First Edition

09 08 07 06 05 04   10 9 8 7 6 5 4 3 2 1

This book is dedicated to:

My wife Christine, whose love and support makes everything possible.

Contents

Preface

In developing background material for a corporate training session on "Avoiding the Traps of Micromanagement," I found zero publications on this specific topic. A key word search of various Internet engines yielded over twenty-five thousand hits on *micromanagement*. There were many articles and references, yet no publications. Obviously, it is an important topic of interest, but no one has given it formal definition or delved into corrective strategies.

This book defines micromanagement, separates illusion from reality, offers diagnostic tools, and identifies corrections. It is intended to offer structure to the discussion.

A book like this could only be written as a collaborative effort. It reflects a lifetime of experience combined with valuable input from many knowledgeable people who were willing to share their thoughts and ideas. I gained tremendous insight from all of those who were willing to contribute information and anecdotes to this manuscript.

I would especially like to thank my wife, Chris, whose collaboration was immense. Her support and editing skills have taken this from a series of disjointed thoughts to a book with some meaningful structure. She functions as coauthor and keeps me focused.

Mickey Beatty has once again proven invaluable to another publication. This is the sixth book, none of which would exist if it wasn't for her help, dedication, and flexibility. She creates the manuscript, meets the deadlines, and somehow makes sense of my ramblings.

Katherine Wilson, Ph.D., was very helpful in structuring and evaluating the Micromanagement Survey. She kept me honest. She made sure that I wasn't just creating a survey to create the results I wanted. She is a talented lady.

I would like to give special thanks to all who contributed information, including the following:

Lani Arredondo	John Gamble	Ron Melchiorre
Karen Bishop	Tim Green	Kevin Moody
Steve Boedigheimer	Judy Hannan	Julie Sharpe
Joe Bork	Bill Herdman	Deb Smith
Kevin Brady	William Lampton	Norah Walsh
Tom Butler	Wendy MacColl	Mary K. Decker
Ken Futch	Bill McIlwaine	Paul Halverson

And all those who wish to remain anonymous!

To all of you: Your wisdom and creativity were extremely valuable.

The Micromanagement Survey contained in this manuscript was possible because of the efforts of many people who were willing not only to share their perceptions but also to encourage others to respond to the survey. To all of you who participated, a heartfelt thank you.

I would also like to thank both Steven Piersanti, Jeevan Sivasubramaniam, and the many other professionals within Berrett-Koehler. This is my first publication with Berrett-Koehler, and I have found it to be an exceptional organization with a unique and refreshing publishing philosophy. If anyone reading this book has an interest in publishing a business-related book, I would strongly urge you to consider a publishing partnership with Berrett-Koehler. The staff there truly are focused on a world that works for all.

Harry E. Chambers
September, 2004

PART I
Micromanagement

Fact and fiction

Introduction

The term *micromanagement* has become another overused buzzword in today's jargon. For many, it is a pejorative catchall phrase used when they do not like the actions or behaviors of someone in management. It is an often used, yet frequently misunderstood, term. It is much like the word *empowerment*. Everybody believes in empowerment; they are just not quite sure what it means! Nobody wants to be micromanaged, and certainly no one wants to be a micromanager. Everyone knows micromanagement is bad, but they can't actually define it. They just "know it" when it is happening to them.

As you will see throughout this book, the behaviors of micromanagement can be formally defined and the illusion separated from the reality. The circumstances of micromanagement are not limited only to those in formal management positions.

EXPANDING THE PERCEPTION

In the traditional sense, micromanagement is perceived as the negative controlling behaviors of managers or people with power and authority toward others. Front-line managers/ supervisors, team leaders, middle managers, directors, and executives are typically those seen as inflicting micromanagement on the people who report to them. While this is the most common view of micromanagement, it is limited. The behaviors of micromanagement are much deeper and more prevalent, and they are not limited only to managers and their employees.

Some people are considered to be "high-maintenance" by their managers and peers. The factors that result in someone being labeled high-maintenance include significant demands for attention, a need to exercise control, and consistent attempts to exert inappropriate influence over others.

Many of the behaviors of micromanagement experienced in the workplace are duplicated in our personal lives as well. Friendships, marriages, familial, and parent–child relationships all experience the pressures of micromanagement. (While editing this book, my wife, Chris, became convinced that I was writing an autobiography; she would repeatedly look up from her reading and say, "This is you!") If you are good at connecting the dots, you will see the similarity in your work and personal life experiences.

360-DEGREE MICROMANAGEMENT

The behaviors of micromanagement occur in all directions and in many circumstances, including

- employees of managers,

- boards of directors and trustee groups
  of organizational leaders,

- customers of suppliers/vendors,

- suppliers/vendors of customers,

- peer to peer,

- interdepartmental/interteam, and

- personal relationships.

While the list may be endless, other nonmanagement examples include teachers of students, students of teachers, government of people/groups, people/groups of government (e.g., special interest groups), and branches of government of other branches of government.

THE DEGREES AND CONTINUUM

This book will identify four very specific negative behaviors that comprise micromanagement. We will also consider a major contributor, which is the inability to subordinate self. In truth, all of us, managers and nonmanagers alike, have some degree of micromanagement behavior unconsciously ingrained in our personal and professional styles. It is not just about everybody else! The key to dealing with these behaviors in others, and reducing them in ourselves, is being aware of their existence and impact. These behaviors are part of our human experience. They move from normal, acceptable levels to "micro" when they are consistent, predictable, and disruptive.

Interestingly, we are all very good at identifying these behaviors in others, yet we are "selectively blind" to seeing them in ourselves. We judge others harshly for the behaviors and activities we easily rationalize in ourselves.

THE POSITIONING OF THIS BOOK

This manuscript is multidimensional. It views micromanagement from many different perspectives.

Identifying and Defining the Scope

Part I clarifies what micromanagement is as well as what it is not. Definitions, examples, root causes, and the costs of micromanagement are offered to add insight to the discussion.

The MicromanagEE (The Person Being Micromanaged)

Part II identifies specific strategies for dealing with the micromanagement behaviors of others. Whether it is your boss, peers, or people in your personal life, *you do not have to be a victim* of micromanagement. Victims are people who have no options. Your options may be abundant in some circumstances or limited in others, but you are not helpless. Some of the strategies invite you to accommodate the micromanaging to some degree, but they are not intended to just placate or "suck up." As one of the early reviewers of this book, Charlie Dorris, said, "Survival on the job without your soul is not really surviving." This book is not about surrendering; it is about choosing the appropriate response to micromanaged situations.

In the face of intense micromanagement, you may ultimately have to exercise your right to move on. However, before you choose that extreme option, there are other alternatives to consider. The worst thing you can do when facing significant micromanagement is . . . nothing.

You probably cannot alter the micromanaging behaviors of others, but you can certainly change how you react and deal with them. Learn to control what you can.

The MicromanagER

Part III addresses corrective actions that can be implemented to

- avoid becoming a person who micromanages,
- reduce any current micromanagement behaviors,
- repair any damage that you may have done with existing or past behaviors, and
- help all veteran managers and nonmanagers alike who are finding their traditional behaviors and strategies eroding.

Managers of Micromanagers

Part IV addresses those who have a formal stake in attempting to correct the micromanagement behaviors in others.

If you formally manage managers or nonmanagement people who consistently display these behaviors, you will learn strategies and techniques for raising awareness and offering alternatives for correction.

If you are an HR professional, alternative dispute resolution specialist, or anyone who has responsibility for helping others change, cope, or develop responsible options, you will find some valuable tools contained within this book.

PRELIMINARY MICROMANAGEMENT BEHAVIOR INVENTORY

Please complete the following by putting a check mark in all columns that apply. You are being asked to identify the occurrence of these behaviors in three areas: current and past managers, current and past peers/team members, and your own past and present behaviors. Later in this book, when the micromanagement behaviors have been described in more detail, you will have the opportunity to reassess your responses.

■ *Which of the following behaviors are you currently experiencing or have experienced in the past in these areas? (Check all that apply.)*

BEHAVIORS	MANAGERS/ SUPERVISORS	PEERS/ TEAMMATES/ OTHERS	SELF
Dominance, control, or disruption of your time?			
Attempts to impose their will by use of raw power or authority?			
Consistently having to "win"?			

BEHAVIORS	MANAGERS/ SUPERVISORS	PEERS/ TEAMMATES/ OTHERS	SELF
Complete control over "how" things must be done?			
Requiring excessive, unnecessary approvals of tasks or decisions?			
Intense monitoring of your activities?			
Excessive, unnecessary, redundant reporting requirements?			
Refusal to delegate?			
Refusal to accept collaboration?			
Incomplete, unclear or distorted information?			

We will begin in chapter 1 by actually defining the term *micromanagement*, reviewing the survey results concerning the pervasiveness of the issue, introducing the Micromanagement Potential Indicator, and addressing the realities of micromanagement in today's workplace.

You Might Be Micromanaging If . . .

You wrote the book of MBHH (managing by hovering and hounding).

You don't trust your people to do the jobs you hired them to do.

You never take a vacation because "something might happen at work."

You have ever hosted a conference call when on vacation.

You pass notes to employees under the restroom stall door.

You put a time clock on the restroom door.

Employees celebrate your retirement—for months after you leave.

You follow employees during their drive to work in order to find a better route.

You are involved in day-to-day decisions at two or more levels in the organization.

You have ever called an employee who was on vacation to see how things are going.

You believe that allowing employees to make decisions is a threat to your livelihood.

You think that forming teams means employees will gather together while you tell them what you want them to do.

You have received more than one copy of this book . . . anonymously.

1

■　■　■

The Scope of Micromanagement

Just about everyone can identify with the frustrations of being micromanaged. Whether it is their current situation or memories of past challenging experiences, most people believe that they have been under the thumb of someone who micromanages. The following chapters will help to determine whether those perceptions are valid, identify some of the reasons the micromanagement took place, and offer options for dealing with current and future situations.

Perceptions of being micromanaged are sometimes misinterpretations of fairly common circumstances:

- Disagreements
- Being subjected to the influence of others
- Misunderstandings
- Unwanted intrusions into your domain
- Being held accountable

For some people, being micromanaged is a self-fulfilling perception. They do not want to be managed, period! Any attempts to influence their activities or hold them accountable are seen as micro. While most of us have chafed under what we believe is "too close" influence over our activities, it does not necessarily mean that we were being micromanaged.

WHAT IS MICROMANAGEMENT?

Micromanagement is all about interference and disruption. It occurs when influence, involvement, and interaction begin to subtract value from people and processes. It is the perception of inappropriate interference in someone else's activities, responsibilities, decision making, and authority. It can also be any activity that creates interference with process, policies, systems, and procedures. Basically, micromanagement is the excessive, unwanted, counterproductive interference and disruption of people or things.

Micromanagement is a very subjective term. There is a significant gray area between what one person sees as interference and another sees as support and interaction. Participation, guidance, and collaboration, to some, are seen as meddling, manipulation, and excessive control by others. There is a large gap between the perception of the micromanagEE and the micromanagER.

When someone is accused of micromanaging, they often respond, "I'm not micromanaging . . .

I'm only trying to help.

I'm only trying to be sure we're successful.

I'm sharing my experience and knowledge.

I'm just trying to make it easier.

I just want to know what's going on.

I'm only doing what is necessary to ensure success."

In the past, we branded the scarlet letter *A* into people's foreheads who were accused of adultery. Today we tattoo an imaginary scarlet *MM* on the forehead of a manager and others when we don't like what they are doing. Statements such as "I'm being micromanaged" frequently really mean

I don't like the style in which I'm being managed.

I don't like other team members messing in my stuff.

It's not fair when everyone doesn't agree with me.

I'm being managed, and I don't like it.

My boss isn't letting me have my way.

I have to be unhappy about something.

I don't like my manager.

Poor me.

When we don't like something, we label and demonize it. "Micromanagement" has become the trendy, negative, overused label of choice. Just because someone is unhappy with the activity of others doesn't always mean he or she is being micromanaged. In today's workplace, with its ever-escalating tendencies toward whining, blaming, and avoiding responsibility, for many, the statement "I am being micro-managed" is the grown-up equivalent to the eternal teen-age lament of "My parents just don't understand me."

The people being blamed for micromanaging perceive that their interference is minimal if, in fact, it occurs at all. They do not see any problem. Most are shocked if they are openly accused of micromanaging.

The ability to deal with any micromanagement effec-tively is contingent upon our ability to reduce the gap of perception between the micromanagEE and the microman-agER. We have to shrink and lighten the areas of gray!

Question:
When do participation, collaboration, and oversight become micromanagement?

Answer:
When they interfere with performance, quality, and efficiency. When they become barriers to achieve-ment, or impediments to getting things done. Micro-management and micromanagers do not add value to individuals or processes. Regardless of the intent, the results are subtraction, not addition.

Figure 1.1 depicts the transition from adding value to individuals and process toward interference by impeding the efficiency and productivity of individuals and process.

Figure 1.1   The Micromagagement Cascade

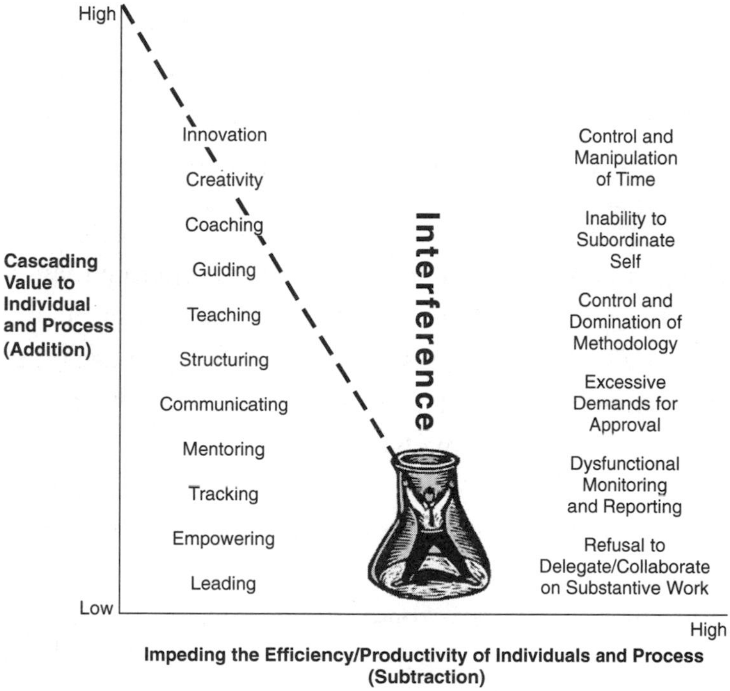

Impeding the Efficiency/Productivity of Individuals and Process
(Subtraction)

The positive contributions such as

innovation	communicating
creativity	mentoring
coaching	tracking
guiding	empowering
teaching	leading
structuring	

give way to

manipulation of time	dominance of self
control of methodology	excessive demands for approval
excessive monitoring and reporting	dysfunctional delegation/ collaboration

The gap between the perceptions of the micromanagER and the micromanagEE is the breeding ground for misunderstanding, morale problems, high frustration, and declining productivity. The broader the gap, the less job satisfaction there is for everyone involved.

The most important factor in dealing with micromanagement and neutralizing its negative impact is to discover precisely when the interference and disruption occurs. Without this discovery, the disconnect in the perceptions of micromanagement will be never-ending. The more accurate and timely the discovery, the quicker and more effectively the damage and debilitating costs of micromanagement can be reduced.

WHAT MICROMANAGEMENT ISN'T

Micromanagement is not abusive management. Behaviors such as temper tantrums, ridicule, public embarrassment, talking behind people's back, inappropriate language, disciplining to punish, intentional untruths, prejudice, deceit, biased performance appraisals, intentional disrespect, demand of blind loyalty, and other similar demonstrations are the realm of abusers, not people who micromanage.

Most micromanagers are well intended and have no interest in demeaning or abusing others.

THE COSTS OF MICROMANAGEMENT

The negative impact of micromanagement permeates to at least four areas: (1) the organization, (2) the micromanagEE, (3) the micromanager, and (4) the customer.

To the Organization

- Retention problems
- Increased levels of unresolved conflict
- Excessive tardiness and absenteeism
- Failure to correct internal deficiencies
- Reduced quality/process improvement
- An increase in lawsuits
- Higher resistance to change initiatives
- Escalations of formal employee complaints

The MicromanagER

- Career stagnation
- Diminished responsiveness
- Becoming a bottleneck
- Increased turnaround/cycle
- Lower productivity from others

- Becoming an impediment to change
- Lack of support/allies
- Personal exposure

The MicromanagEE

- Low morale
- Absence of risk taking
- Lower job satisfaction
- Perceived lack of value
- Diminished initiative and creativity
- Boredom
- Decreased commitment
- Increased resentment

The Customer

- Diminished service levels
- Inflexible policies, procedures, and restraints
- Slow response
- Not being listened to
- Problems lacking priority
- Unnecessary costs due to inefficiencies
- Lack of innovation on "new" offerings
- Loss of individuality/uniqueness/value

THE TWO TIERS OF MICROMANAGEMENT

To enhance our understanding further, it is also appropriate to look at the environment in which micromanagement flourishes. There are two important factors to consider: organizational culture and individual style.

Organizational Culture

Some organizations embed micromanagement behaviors as their normal process of doing business. Typically this behavioral standard is set at the top of the organization and cascades downward as it infects every level. If top leadership demonstrates micromanagement behaviors and reinforces those behaviors in others, micromanagement becomes both the norm and a mimicked style of choice. Managers, would-be managers, and staff-level employees all learn that the way to get ahead around here and keep the peace is to be just like the boss!

Another cultural factor worth mentioning is the emphasis placed on management and staff development. When managers and leaders are not effectively trained in the skills necessary to lead others, or when employees are not trained to work collaboratively, there is a consistent and predictable tendency to gravitate toward the controlling behaviors of micromanagement. Unfortunately, one of the primary reasons that micromanagement has become so prevalent is because people have not been trained to do it differently. Micromanagement becomes the style of default.

Individual Style

Individuals can also move toward micromanagement regardless of the organizational culture. Highly collaborative, interactive team environments can have micromanaging individuals. Even the most enlightened organizations can have individuals whose tendency it is to micromanage other individuals and situations. For some it is a behavior of choice; for many it is both a lack of awareness and training.

In today's workplace, micromanaging individuals are becoming more and more negatively visible.

THE MICROMANAGEMENT SURVEY

How pervasive is the problem of micromanagement?

In a survey conducted by Trinity Solutions, Inc., Peachtree City, Georgia and independently administered by Katherine M. Wilson, Ph.D., we learned from respondents that

79% have experienced micromanagement from their current or past managers.

Of respondents who currently identified themselves as managers (supervisors, team leaders, middle managers, executives):

27% said they are currently being micromanaged by their manager;

71% said they had been micromanaged by previous managers;

62% stated they had considered changing jobs because of being micromanaged;

32% stated they had actually changed jobs because of being micromanaged;

73% said that being micromanaged has interfered with their job performance;

77% said their morale has been impacted negatively by being micromanaged;

19% stated they were currently being micromanaged by others (not someone they report to directly);

47% stated they have been micromanaged by others in the past.

Of respondents who currently identified themselves as nonmanagers:

37% said they are currently being micromanaged by their manager;

67% said they have been micromanaged by previous managers;

69% stated they have considered changing jobs because of being micromanaged;

36% stated they have actually changed jobs because of being micromanaged;

71% said that being micromanaged has interfered with their job performance;

85% said their morale has been impacted negatively by being micromanaged;

23% stated they are currently being micromanaged by others (not someone they report to directly);

53% stated they have been micromanaged by others in the past.

The disconnect:

22% of managers acknowledge currently demonstrating some of the micromanagement behaviors;

48% of managers acknowledge having demonstrated these behaviors in the past;

38% of nonmanagers acknowledge demonstrating some of the micromanagement behaviors either currently or in the past;

91% of managers are unaware of employees changing jobs because of their micromanagement style and behaviors.

What can we learn from the survey?

- Micromanagement is pervasive.

- Both managers and nonmanagers experience it.

- Managers and nonmanagers alike demonstrate the behaviors.

- People change jobs because of it.

- Productivity is reduced because of it.

- Morale is negatively impacted because of it.

- Few people think they are doing it.

- Most people are oblivious to the negative impact their micromanagement behaviors have on others.

- Over a third of managers believe it is what their organization wants them to do.

- Most people think everyone else is doing it, *but not them.*

The Micromanagement Survey Results/ Specific Behaviors

The following responses are ranked in order of affirmative responses.

■ *Have you experienced these micromanagement behaviors from managers?*

BEHAVIOR	MANAGERS' RANKING	NONMANAGERS' RANKING
1. Control over methodologies or "how" things are done	1	1
2. Unnecessary/excessive requirements for approvals	3	2
3. Exercise of raw power/ imposing their will	5	3
4. Dominance and control over time	2	4
5. Excessive monitoring and reporting	4	5

■ *Have you experienced these micromanagement*
behaviors in peers, team members, or other
nonmanagers?

BEHAVIOR	MANAGERS' RANKING	NONMANAGERS' RANKING
1. Refusal to collaborate	1	1
2. Dominance and control over time	2	2
3. Control over methodologies or "how" things are done	3	3
4. Having to win	5	4
5. Incomplete sharing of information	4	5

WHY DOES MICROMANAGEMENT OCCUR?

People who are perceived to be micromanaging are typically judged harshly. They are believed to be control freaks
lacking trust and confidence in others. Their behaviors are
assumed to be rooted in insecurity and arrogance. The behavior patterns of micromanagers seem to imply that

> they believe they are smarter and more capable than
> those around them, and

> they must keep a close eye on everyone else to ensure
> that things are done correctly.

Although these perceptions may have some legitimacy, they are often simplistic, knee-jerk attempts at criticizing and labeling behaviors that we find uncomfortable. The vast majority of time micromanagement is shrouded in unawareness (as our survey indicated). For some, it may be a conscious disregard for how their behaviors impact others. If so, it is an expensive disregard with the toll on productivity and morale. Invest your efforts in addressing the behaviors of micromanagement, and avoid getting bogged down in petty, self-serving labeling. We all demonstrate the behaviors to some degree, but when we do it, it is certainly not due to insecurity, arrogance, or a pathological need to exercise control.

Those who micromanage are not bad people with diabolical intentions. In some cases, it is learned behavior that has been successful in the past. Often people do not know how to influence others successfully without becoming "micro" in their attempts. In the absence of training and development, we all tend to mimic the past behaviors of those who seemed to be successful. Many of today's unacceptable micromanagement behaviors are, in actuality, remnants of the encouraged behaviors of past autocratic, authoritarian environments.

The focus of this book is how to reduce our own micromanagement behaviors and respond effectively to those behaviors in others. To broaden our understanding, it is appropriate to look at some of the root causes of these behaviors.

A FORMULA FOR CAUSES
OF MICROMANAGEMENT

The actual root causes of micromanagement can be displayed in a formula:

$$Mm = Fr + Cm + Cf$$

In other words: Micromanagement = Fear + Comfort + Confusion.

All three components contribute to micromanagement. For some people, it is a blend of all three; others may be influenced by only one or two of the root causes. All are the drivers of micromanagement. Many of these factors will be discussed in greater depth in succeeding chapters.

Fear

The behaviors of micromanagement are strongly influenced by fear. In fact, much of micromanagement is an attempt to avoid a possible negative outcome. This may be a specific, clearly identified fear or a general foreboding that things could potentially "go wrong." The fear may be targeted inward toward self or externally toward others. Others interpret the micromanager's behaviors as an indication of low trust and perception of incompetence in them.

✳ *Fear is a powerful motivator of behavior.*

Some of the fear factors contributing to micromanagement are as follows:

- Lack of confidence in personal ability to influence others

- Potential failure of others

- Public embarrassment or being made to look bad

- Being left out of the loop

- Loss of recognition or credit for achievement

- Loss of influence over the final outcome

- Irrelevance

- Territorial infringement

- Threat of others' competence

Comfort

In many circumstances, it is just plain easier to micromanage. It is comfortable to continue to do things the way you have always done them and disregard input from others. Change causes discomfort.

It is easier and more comfortable to correct and direct others than it is to correct and direct self. Often people who want to give advice to others on how to lead their lives, or do their jobs, or fix their problems are those whose personal situations are in chaos. Did you ever notice how easy it is to quit somebody else's job, divorce somebody else's mate, or tell somebody else what he or she should do to be successful? People who micromanage avoid the risk of self-accountability by submerging themselves in the activities of others.

✳ *For some micromanagers, it is more comfortable and fun to be on a controlling power trip.*

Comfort has many factors, including these:

- Self-reliance (If you want it done well, do it yourself.)
- Lack of patience
- The illusion of activity (It is easier to look busy than it is to be truly effective.)
- Risk avoidance
- Exercise of raw power (Some people control and micromanage because they can!)
- Familiarity of crisis, escalated stress, and increased pressure
- Lack of flexibility (Rigidity is easy. Flexibility, accepting change, and considering exceptions to policies and procedures are often uncomfortable.)

Confusion

Confusion reigns when priorities, objectives, and goals are not clearly identified, communicated, or accurately comprehended. Confusion creates unfocused activity or inactivity; in some cases, it freezes people in place. People who micromanage are quick to step in and fill any perceived void. They believe their activity is necessary to gain order and stability. Confusion provides many people with an open invitation to micromanage.

Interestingly, this is a chicken-and-egg situation. Micromanagers are not clear in establishing roles, responsibilities, accountability, and expectations; thus, they create the confusion. They then intensify their micromanagement behaviors to correct a problem of their own creation. Talk about a lose/lose situation! They contribute to confusion and then feel compelled to "fix it."

Often micromanagers hire the "best and brightest," yet they do not allow these people to be the best and brightest. The cause is frequently due to unclear roles and responsibilities, coupled with a reluctance to give them the authority. How can people do well that which they do not know to do?

People who micromanage cannot tell you what they actually want, yet they can tell you what they don't. They can tell you what it isn't, but not what it is. While they cannot really clarify their expectation, they will just know it when they see it.

✳ *Confusion reigns when the criteria for judging progress and outcomes is not clear.*

Here are some typical examples of confusion:

- Failure to enable authority (Responsibility and accountability without authority)
- Lack of clearly defined outcomes/expectation
- An unawareness of shifts in priorities and deadlines
- No mechanisms for evaluating progress
- Failure to communicate "why"
- Decisions without explanation
- Lack of clear problem diagnosis

Fear, comfort, and confusion stimulate the behaviors of micromanagement. They also provide validation and justification for those who micromanage.

ARE YOU A MICROMANAGER?

The following indicator was developed by Trinity Solutions, Inc. The indicator is offered to help participants determine their own potential for demonstrating the behavior of micromanagement.

The value of this instrument is determined by your honesty. Please do not select the socially desirable answer. Choose the response that accurately describes you.

The Micromanagement Potential Indicator

Please select an "a" or "b" response for each statement. Choose the statement that best applies to you.

---

1. I prefer a work environment that is
    a. Structured   b. Unstructured

2. My work relationships tend to be
    a. Formal   b. Informal

3. I offer input on how others can best utilize their time
    a. Frequently   b. Infrequently

4. The phrase that best describes me is
    a. "Gotta win"   b. "Doing the best I can"

5. My thoughts and comments about the work of others tend to be
    a. Critical   b. Not critical

6. The phrase that best describes me is
    a. "Hate to lose"   b. "Doing the best I can"

7. I prefer others to
    a. Follow directions   b. Exercise creativity

8. I need others to
    a. Keep me informed   b. Work independently

9. People work better when
    a. Closely monitored   b. Trained and
                                    empowered

The Micromanagement Potential Indicator *(continued)*
Please select an "a" or "b" response for each statement.
Choose the statement that best applies to you.

---

10. In making decisions, I want people to
    a. Seek my guidance/   b. Act on their own
       approval   and keep me
                                  informed

11. In completing tasks, I want people to
    a. Follow existing methods   b. Create methods
                                    that are best for
                                    them

12. Meetings are
    a. Essential to good   b. Effective only when
       communication and   necessary
       performance

13. I think others perceive that I share information
    a. Only when necessary   b. Open and freely

14. I break the rules or ignore policy
    a. Only when necessary   b. Never

15. When my expectations are unmet, I typically react
    a. Strongly/vocally   b. Passively/ silently

16. I consider myself a change agent
    a. Yes   b. No

17. I think other people perceive my attitude toward
    change as
    a. Accepting   b. Resisting

18. When my duties and responsibilities have been changed, I
    a. Welcome the challenge
    b. Feel like I am being punished

19. I like to do things
    a. My way
    b. In accordance with policies and procedures

20. I typically view change as
    a. Gain
    b. Loss

21. I think others see me as
    a. Unpredictable
    b. Predictable

22. I tend to
    a. Discard things easily
    b. Be a pack rat

23. Tradition and consistency are
    a. Nice
    b. Very important to me

24. My attitude toward a lateral move would be
    a. Willing to consider
    b. Doubtful . . . why move laterally?

25. When asked to do something I don't agree with, I
    a. Disregard my own perceptions and follow through
    b. Think it's unfair and try to change the task

26. I change my appearance
    a. Often
    b. Rarely

27. Change is necessary
    a. Less for me
    b. More for everyone else

The Micromanagement Potential Indicator *(continued)*
Please select an "a" or "b" response for each statement.
Choose the statement that best applies to you.

---

28. When I am threatened by something, I
    a. Speak out to address it   b. Remain quiet and
    internalize my
    feelings

29. People who drive change are my
    a. Ally   b. Adversary

30. I tend to be
    a. Creative   b. Consistent

31. People who see things differently than I do are
    a. Misguided   b. Interesting

32. I prefer to work
    a. Independently   b. In teams/with others

33. When others offer comments concerning my tasks,
    responsibilities, and performance, I
    a. Tolerate them   b. Welcome them

34. If a task can be shared or assigned to others, I would
    rather
    a. Do it myself   b. Teach others to
    do it

35. If you want something done right
    a. Do it yourself   b. Invite others' input
    and creativity

36. When others need help, I typically
    a. Encourage them to   b. Offer assistance
       seek help from others   myself

37. In a situation of potential delegation, I
    a. Usually think it's   b. Consider it an
       quicker to do it myself   opportunity to help
                                  others grow and
                                  develop

38. I can achieve more
    a. Working on my own   b. Working in concert
                               with others

39. My attitude regarding working in teams or in groups is
    a. "A camel is a racehorse   b. "None of us is as
       designed by a committee"   smart as all of us"

40. I would rather win an Olympic gold medal in
    a. An individual event   b. A team sport

41. If given the opportunity to assign tasks to others, I
    would initially give away
    a. Tasks I was bored with   b. Tasks that others could
       or didn't like   perhaps do better

42. I would rather
    a. Write a best-selling novel   b. Direct an Academy
                                        Award–winning movie

43. I think other people would describe my working
    style as
    a. Solitary   b. Interactive

The Micromanagement Potential Indicator *(continued)*

Please select an "a" or "b" response for each statement. Choose the statement that best applies to you.

---

44. When others in my group or team do not support my ideas, my first reaction is to
    a. Withhold support of their ideas (an eye for an eye)   b. Seek common ground

45. My interpretation of the 80/20 rule would be
    a. 80% of the work is done by 20% of the people   b. 80% of what I do could be done by others

---

SCORING THE MICROMANAGEMENT INDICATOR

Section I (Questions 1 through 15)

Please count your responses for the first fifteen statements.

"a" Totals _____   "b" Totals _____

Section II (Questions 16 through 30)

Please do the same for the next fifteen statements.

"a" Totals _____   "b" Totals _____

Section III (Questions 31 through 45)

Please do the same for the last fifteen statements.

"a" Totals _____   "b" Totals _____

DETERMINING THE MEANING

Section I: Control Factors

Control factors have to do with your preference for being in control and having others be responsive to you. This reflects the tendency to exercise active, overt influence over people and tasks.

More than eight "a" scores in this grouping indicate a tendency toward exercising significant control and influence. This figure may indicate the potential to micromanage tasks and people.

Eleven or more "a" responses in this grouping would indicate a high probability of current micromanagement behaviors. There is a great likelihood that others may perceive you to have a definite need to exercise unnecessary control.

Seven or fewer "a" responses would indicate that the potential for micromanaging is less likely.

Section II: Familiarity Factors

Familiarity factors have to do with the preference for consistency, the status quo, or low to moderate change environments.

People with eight or more "b" scores in this grouping prefer consistency. They are less likely to initiate change and more likely to move slowly in the face of change. This would indicate the potential to demonstrate a significant level of micromanagement behaviors, especially in maintaining familiar methods and historical patterns.

Eleven or more "b" responses in this grouping would indicate a high probability of micromanaging behaviors. There is a strong likelihood that others may perceive you to be inflexible and unresponsive to others creativity and initiative taking.

Seven or fewer "b" responses would indicate that the tendency toward micromanaging is less likely.

Section III: Collaboration/Delegation Factors

These statements have to do with the preference of working interactively with others or working in a solitary style. This indicates a comfort level with assigning work and sharing responsibilities with others.

Eight or more "a" responses would indicate less of a preference for working in teams or interactive groups and more of a tendency to work in a solitary environment. Given the choice, they are less likely to invite collaboration or delegate tasks to others.

Eleven or more "a" responses in this grouping would indicate an increased probability of micromanaging behaviors. There is a high likelihood that others may perceive that you place low value on the input and abilities of others and want to maintain personal influence over outcomes.

Seven or fewer "a" responses or eight or more "b" responses would indicate that the tendency toward micromanaging is less likely.

Total Scoring

Please add your total numbers from each section.

Section I   Control   "a" responses _____
Section II   Familiarity   "b" responses _____
Section III   Collaboration   "a" responses _____
                               TOTAL   _____

Totals of 11 or less: Please get a second opinion! Denial or sociable desirability may have influenced your responses. Most people who have a tendency toward micromanagement are not aware they are doing it.

Totals of 21 or less: Low probability of micromanagement behaviors. If accurate responses were selected, micromanagement tendencies are not in evidence.

Totals in the range of 22–32: Would indicate a medium to high probability that significant micromanagement behaviors are either currently being demonstrated or could be in the future. The tendency to micromanage may be inconsistent; however, there is a high probability that interference with or disruption of others either is or will occur. There is a medium likelihood that contributing to the low morale of others is or will occur.

Scores of 33 and above: This is considered the "red zone." These scores indicate a high probability that significant micromanagement behaviors are currently impacting others. Substantial interference with and disruption of others productivity is evident, probably to a career-damaging level. The negative impact on the morale of others is great and retention problems are likely to occur.

If you have scored in the red zone and continue to adamantly believe that you are not micromanaging, please access a dictionary and look up the meaning of the word *denial*.

As we move to chapter 2, we look at the primary factor that drives the behaviors of micromanagers: the inability to subordinate self.

You Might Be Micromanaging If . . .

People return from lunch to find that you have finished their project for them or assigned it to someone else.

You instruct others on how to be better organized while your own office is in chaos.

You are constantly directing others to fix problems and put out fires that you created yourself.

Delegating authority to others is as painful as gnawing off one of your own limbs.

You ever told someone, "You are responsible for this, but before you make any decisions, be sure to check with me."

Someone asks, "Why?" and your response is "Because I told you so."

2

■ ■ ■

Team "Me"
Putting the I *in Micro*

The engine that pulls the train of micromanagement is the inability to subordinate self. *Subordination of self* is the setting aside of personal perceptions, opinions, and, at times, self-interest for the greater good or the best interest of others. Unfortunately, people who micromanage usually think it is all about "them." They lack the ability to take themselves out of the equation. *Me, my*, and *I* are the micromanager's favorite pronouns.

In its most egregious form, the inability to subordinate self results in personal or organizational corruption. Loosely defined, *corruption* is the promotion of self at the expense of all other considerations. In its most extreme, it is rooted in greed, avarice, and self-promotion. It is one of the primary contributors to fraud and dishonesty. The excessive behaviors that brought us Enron, Tyco, Global Crossings, Wall Street corruption, and so forth, are extreme examples of the inability and unwillingness of individuals and leadership groups to subordinate self. This trait alone is arguably the single most responsible factor for the erosion of trust in today's workplace. Many micromanagement factors diminish trust, and this is the most pervasive.

In its more common forms, this trait of micromanagement results in the behaviors of "Team Me." "What's good for me is good for the organization and everybody in it, and even if it's not, it should be." It reflects an inflated value of one's own opinion, intellect, knowledge, decisions, expertise, and analysis. The celebration of self is conjoined with the devaluation of these same factors in others. In total, the failure to subordinate self and the interference and disruption it causes are among the most career damaging for micromanagers themselves and the most frustrating to the people around them.

Some typical examples of this trait are detailed in the following sections of this chapter.

NOT LISTENING

A common complaint lodged against people being accused of micromanagement is their unwillingness to listen. Listening is an "other-focused" activity. The inability to subordinate self inherently lessens the value of others. "Why listen when I already know the answer? If I am always right, then listening to others is a colossal waste of time!"

THE RAW EXERCISE OF POWER

In the micromanagement survey, 52% of current managers and 60% of nonmanagers stated they have experienced managers exercising their raw power and imposing their will. It can be very self-rewarding to flex your muscles and prove to people that you have authority and are willing to assert it. Although at times the use of authority is appropriate, productive, and necessary, in many situations micromanagers assert their authority just because they can. The alpha dog feels the need to assert dominance and force the other dogs to submit.

Micromanager Charles

Charles was promoted to CEO of the FAA (Financial, Accounting, Auditing) division of a major pharmaceutical company. He relocated from the corporate headquarters in the Midwest to take over the FAA division in Miami, Florida. The division employed 2,500 people and was highly visible, efficient, and profitable for the company. The previous divisional CEO was promoted to CFO of the parent company and was considered by most to be the heir apparent for the company's top job. The divisional FAA CEO job is a highly sought-after position, and there was intense competition among midlevel and senior executives within the company. Charles won the competition and appears destined for even greater things.

Upon assuming his new position, one of the immediate changes that Charles announced was the physical relocation of the division. He was moving the operation lock, stock, and barrel to a location approximately twenty-five miles north of Miami. He cited as justification for the move such things as the heavy traffic congestion, difficult commutes, and the expense of a prime downtown location. Perhaps it was just coincidence that the new location was less than eight miles from Charles's new home in a very exclusive resort community.

When the relocation was announced, it received mixed reviews from employees. Some people welcomed the move to the new location because it would be more convenient for them, whereas others would experience significant disruption to their routines with new extended morning and evening commutes. As with all change, for some there was gain; for others there was loss.

Coinciding with the move, Charles announced a new flextime policy for all employees. The division's employees would be permitted, with the approval of their manager, to designate a work schedule that would balance convenience and productivity. Everyone was required to put in a nine-hour day (including an hour for lunch), but the nine hours could begin at any time between 7:00 and 9:00 A.M., provided there was at least minimal coverage at all times. It was deemed important to have some employees from each department working the latest block of hours from 9:00 to 6:00 to accommodate the one-hour time difference with corporate headquarters located in the Central Time Zone. Someone must always be available to respond to late-day requests form the home office.

The relocation went reasonably well, and the flextime policy was very popular. However, the ship soon hit an iceberg. People who worked directly for Charles began to experience less control over their time, a demand to work excessive hours, and an erosion of their decision-making authority.

Two years after the relocation, a series of events occurred that dramatically altered the organization and reinforced the perception of Charles being a micromanager. One morning at 7:00, Charles placed a call to the tax audit department, asking to speak to the manager. He was told that the manager did not arrive until 8:00 A.M. Somewhat frustrated, Charles left a message that the manager was to call him immediately upon arrival. When the manager arrived, the call was placed, and Charles requested some very specific information concerning a recent audit conducted with the foreign subsidiary's office. He was told that Krista, the senior auditor in charge of that specific audit, was not due in until 9:00 A.M. Charles was extremely upset that the information he required was not readily available. He left his office and went down to the internal audit department and, in his opinion, found that "nobody was there." (In fact, 70% of the employees were present. In accordance with existing guidelines, only 30% of the internal audit employees began their workday between 8:00 and 9:00.) The real meaning of "nobody was there" was "the person I wanted wasn't there." In a poorly disguised, controlled rage, Charles walked through the entire building observing what he believed to be an unacceptable lack of employees present and available to work. (He saw what he wanted to see.)

Upon returning to his office, he called an emergency meeting with his leadership staff and demanded that the working hours for the organization be changed immediately. His statement was "I get here at 7:00 in the morning, and so can everybody else. This is not a country club. From now on I want everyone here no later than 8:00 A.M."

The leadership staff was quick to identify a number of problems that might occur, not the least of which was the lack *of coverage during the end of the day. It was pointed out that responses to inquiries from headquarters may be delayed if people worked only from 8:00 to 5:00 (actually 7:00 to 4:00 in the Central Time Zone). Unwilling to back down, Charles stated that headquarters could survive if their end-of-day requests were not addressed until the following morning. (Previously this had been a primary concern of his.) He was adamant in enforcing the new work hours policy. Even in the face of logic and reason, he was unable to deviate from his impulsive reaction or reconsider his initial decision.*

The human resources director experienced a meltdown upon learning of the new directive. She cited the importance of maintaining the previous commitment, the obvious negative impact on employee morale, and the reality of potential lawsuits over the change. She advised Charles that his new policy was unwise. Charles still refused to budge. The HR director's opinion was supported by both the corporate HR and legal departments. Charles was told that he could not mandate a policy change; he could only "recommend" that all employees start work by 8:00 A.M.

As a result, Charles issued a definitive "recommendation" that the core working hours for all FAA divisional employees be changed. Managers at all levels were strongly encouraged to deny any requests for variations except in the most extreme circumstances. A few managers perceived that since it was a recommendation and not a policy, there was some wiggle room, and they chose not to implement Charles's recommendation; however, they soon suffered various forms of retaliation. Most managers did comply. The primary reason for doing so was not agreement with the change, but it was deemed an unhealthy career decision to buck Charles. The result was the flextime policy was neutered. Thirty percent of the employees experienced an unpleasant disruption to their lifestyles. Along with the negative impact on morale, the new circumstances resulted in decreased efficiency in the work of the division and a significant erosion of trust. A previously stable workforce began to experience retention problems. The home office noted a drop in internal customer service, and the HR director feared her job may be in jeopardy.

Charles did prove that he was the boss. He inserted himself into a situation inappropriately and mandated a disruptive change that was probably neither necessary nor in the best interest of the organization. Why did he do all this? Because he could! It was an exercise of raw power.

The alpha dog prevailed.

LACK OF SUPPORT/COMPLIANCE WITH POLICIES, DIRECTIVES, AND GUIDELINES

People who micromanage often vocalize their personal disagreement with many of the policies, procedures, strategies, plans, and so forth, they are required to implement. When something comes down from on high, they are quick to criticize the action. Their criticism and disagreement do not go to the decision makers but instead are directed toward their peers or the people who work for them directly. They openly share their perception that they would do it differently and much better. Micromanagers are quick to spread the poison.

They make statements such as

This is what we are being told to do, but I think it's wrong.

I don't like this any more than you do, but here's what we have to do . . . .

This is how we are being told to do this, but I think it would be better if we did. . . .

This is the stupidest thing we've ever done. My idea would have been much better.

Obviously, if someone is asked to implement something that is illegal, unethical, or immoral, it is appropriate and necessary to show opposition. However, barring those extremes, the inability to subordinate self results in a continuation of opposition based on opinion. Micromanagers expect others to suck it up, stifle their disagreement, and move on—yet they are not willing or able to do so themselves.

Micromanagers have a penchant for positioning themselves to be able to say, "I told you so." If something does not go exactly as planned or result in the perfect outcome, they are quick to point out that their idea was better or they could have done it more successfully. Micromanagers are the Monday morning quarterbacks of the workplace.

In extreme circumstances, micromanagers will withhold support or engage in malicious compliance to create a less than perfect outcome. They may position themselves actually to have a stake in failure. When something is not successful, they get to be right!

By continuing to demonstrate and/or vocalize their disagreement with ongoing initiatives, micromanagers encourage the people around them, or those they directly influence, to do the same. This approach not only positions others to appear oppositional within their area of influence; it spreads the poison of conspiracy.

Some of the explicit or implicit messages:

Maybe if we delay, they will change their mind.

I wouldn't be unhappy if this initiative failed miserably.

I guess we have to do this, but let's not make it a high priority.

They will learn the hard way that they should have listened to me.

BLAMING OTHERS

The fear and comfort of self-protection frequently encourage the deflection of responsibility and accountability. A survival skill for many people who micromanage is "Always have something or somebody else to blame." Micromanagers assume the defense of "Don't shoot me—I'm only the piano player." They distance themselves from responsibility, especially with unpopular or controversial issues.

Micromanagers in formal positions of leadership try to separate themselves from other layers of management. Quick to state, "They are making me/us do this," they refuse to acknowledge that there is no "they." The formal micromanager is a part of "they."

PERSONALIZING DISAGREEMENT

Micromanagers feel perfectly justified in disagreeing with others, yet they take it personally when others disagree with them. Disagreeing, playing the devil's advocate, or offering an alternative is seen by micromanagers as their legitimate birthright. However, it is being negative, disrespectful, disloyal, or interfering when others do it to them. Micromanagers believe that their opinions, preferences, intellect, analysis, and strategies are right, and any reasonably intelligent person would be in agreement with them. Therefore, disagreements become personal very quickly. The inability to subordinate self also demands that all disagreements and conflicts must be "won," and it is important that others know they have "lost."

INABILITY TO PICK BATTLES

The ballad of "The Gambler" by Kenny Rogers contains the famous line "You gotta know when to hold 'em, know when to fold 'em, know when to walk away, know when to run." Micromanagers did not get this memo! They have difficulty determining when something just isn't worth the debate or disagreement. They do not know the difference between a burnt marshmallow and a four-alarm raging fire. They react to everything with the same high intensity.

Perhaps compromise is seen as weakness, and stubbornness or intransigence as great strength. It is as if accepting someone else's input equals personal devaluation and is a battle that must be fought. Letting someone else win or choosing not to pursue a minor issue somehow becomes a loss of face.

LACK OF AFTERTHOUGHT OR RECONSIDERATION

Once a position is taken, it is very difficult for micromanaging types to back off or reconsider. As in the earlier example of the alpha dog Charles, even in the face of valid and rational reasoning, he displayed the inability to reassess the initial decision.

What micromanagers see as great strength (staying the course, being unwilling to bend, refusing to yield to pressure, etc.) is interpreted by others as shallow, weak, immature, and irrational. This behavior perpetuates the assumption that micromanagers are fearful and threatened by others' competence and creativity.

IMPEDIMENTS TO CHANGE

People who micromanage tend to be big supporters of change . . . for everyone else. It is very comfortable to subscribe change for other people, other departments, and other processes. Micromanagers interpret their own need to change from a very narrow perspective. "How does this impact me, my area of responsibility, my level of influence and comfort?"

The criteria used to assess change are as follows:

Is this good for me?

Is this something I agree with?

Does this lessen the impact I have on the process?

How does it make my department/group/team look?

Does this take me out of my comfortable patterns of behavior?

Does this alter my visibility, access, or ability to derive credit?

RE-CREATION OF SELF

Micromanagers' high value of self contributes to the intentional or unintentional favoring of people who are most like them. They promote, support, gather round, treat well, and offer opportunity to people who look, think, talk, and act just like them.

✳ *In the realm of the micromanager, it is difficult to be different.*

Diversity is not a valued concept for micromanagers. They pay a high price for their lack of appreciation of the differences in those around them. Gravitating toward people who have a thought process reflective of their own does not encourage alternative thinking, and they ultimately deny themselves the opportunity of seeing things through different eyes. To the micromanager, the historical Indian philosophy of "Before you judge someone else, walk a mile in their moccasins" really translates into "Everybody's moccasins should be just like mine."

The re-creation of self is experienced very intensely in organizations where the culture of micromanagement has become embedded. When the top management demonstrates the behaviors of micromanagement, others mimic those actions because they are the behaviors that get them noticed. The people at the top grow and develop the people who are most like them. The science of cloning is really not new; many organizations have been cloning micromanagers for years!

HISTORICAL FOCUS

People who micromanage demonstrate repetitive, historical patterns. The past and what they have experienced dictates the present and the future. The inability to subordinate self makes micromanagers place extreme value on their own history and experience, and they are dismissive of these factors in others. Learning from history is important. Continuously reliving or re-creating history is fixating.

This historical focus demonstrates itself in a number of ways, including the style of problem solving and the perpetuation of existing relationships.

Problem Solving

When micromanagers address problems or crises, their initial response is to revisit the way "they" have always dealt with similar issues in the past. In presenting strategies or actions, they will make statements such as

Here's how I have dealt with this in the past;

Here's what I have seen work well in the past;

This is what I have found to be the best way to deal with something like this.

When past experiences become the dominant influence over today's and tomorrow's actions, the same mistakes are repeated. The same problems have to be addressed over and over.

Perpetuating Existing Relationships

Micromanagers place high value on their past historical relationships. When micromanagers change jobs, they will bring past associates with them, if at all possible. Many people have been in the painful situation of being denied mobility or advancement when their new boss brings in past associates from the outside, rather than promoting from within.

✹ *Ongoing relationships are very important; however, there must be a balance between these and new ones.*

Existing vendor and supplier relationships are often disrupted when micromanagers assume responsibility and want to revert back to "the people we have always done business with."

How many times does the micromanager ride in as "the new sheriff in town" and bring his or her own posse?

ENTITLEMENT

The inability to subordinate self drives the micromanagers to believe they are entitled to dominate and have others yield to them. Perhaps it is another birthright! If they do not agree with something, they are entitled to do it their way. If they do not like a change, they are entitled to resist it. The policies, rules, and procedures are important and everyone should comply—except them. They are entitled to be the exception.

THE BLACK HOLE OF DELEGATION AND COLLABORATION

The inability to subordinate self is very evident in the issues of delegation and collaboration. The micromanagement survey yielded these findings:

- 40% of current managers and 43% of nonmanagers have experienced managers who refused to delegate.
- 43% of current managers and 44% of nonmanagers have experienced peers, team members, and associates who refused to collaborate.

The importance of compliance or the quality of the outcome is often the excuse used by micromanagers to defend their lack of delegation and collaboration. They see themselves as possessing special knowledge or skills that preclude the involvement of others. When they do delegate or invite collaboration, they do it ineffectively or perhaps as a tool of manipulation.

Methods of Ineffective Delegation/Collaboration

The following is a summarization of at least six different strategies in dysfunctional delegation and collaboration practiced by micromanagers. Some are conscious and planned; some may be unintentional. All are counter-productive.

- **Delegation or collaboration of nothing** Keeping close control, not letting others in
- **Incomplete or piecemeal delegation/collaboration** Segmenting or compartmentalizing the involvement of others; not allowing anyone else to have a complete view of the entire picture
- **Fluff or busywork** Giving away the things they do not like to do or wasting other people's time instead of their own
- **Delegation/collaboration without authority** Giving away the task without the authority for decision making
- **Delegation/collaboration without training** Assigning a new task without the training to do it effectively
- **Delegation/collaboration to "duck" negative accountability** Giving away or inviting involvement on high-risk tasks that are likely to go bad; demonstrating a high willingness to set others up for failure

Defending the Micromanager's Border

Delegation and collaboration extend to others the opportunity to enter the domain of the micromanager. This is a very threatening circumstance. Others may have a new and better idea, discover current inefficiencies, dig up the well-hidden skeletons of the past, or ask questions that the micromanager may not be able to answer.

High Frustration of Not Being Used to Potential

Severe damage is caused when a thoroughbred racehorse is used to pull a plow. The same holds true in a working relationship when a micromanager does not value the ability of others. Ongoing conflict and discontent can cause people to pursue opportunities elsewhere.

Failure to Grow a Replacement Crop

Succession planning and promotional planning are limited when no one is given meaningful tasks to prepare for future assignments. Organizations may be forced to hire outside people with skills that could have been developed within the company.

Boredom and Burnout

Today is as good as it is going to get! Without delegation and collaboration, nothing changes for anyone. People do not get burned out by working hard; they get burned out by doing the same things over and over. Effective delegation and collaboration shrinks repetition.

Cynicism and Skepticism

Cynicism becomes rampant when a micromanager refuses to delegate or collaborate. It reinforces perceptions that micromanagers are control freaks who do not trust the people around them.

If delegation and collaboration are offered, the question becomes, Why? Why this? Why me? Why now? They search for the trap. Doubt and distrust abound in environments of micromanagement.

Micromanagement Assessment

■ *Is inability to subordinate self an issue?*

	YES	No
1. Do you feel compelled to win most disagreements or conflicts?		
2. Do you expect people to do what you tell them to do? (Because you are the boss?)		
3. Have you ever exercised raw power or authority just because you could?		
4. Are you able to support initiatives even when you disagree?		
5. Have you ever engaged in malicious compliance?		

	YES	No
6. Have you ever acted inappropriately because others deserved it?		
7. Has blaming others become a comfortable option?		
8. Do you have the ability to discern which "battles" need to be engaged?		
9. Are you able to admit when you are wrong or reconsider an unwise position/decision?		
10. Are you able to encourage the "difference" in others?		
11. Do you overcome the temptation to allow past experiences to dominate current problems and solutions?		
12. Are your important work relationships inclusive of new people, vendors, and suppliers and not limited almost exclusively by historical experiences and relationships?		

Any "yes" responses for questions 1 through 8 and "no" responses for questions 9 through 12 indicate opportunities for self-evaluation and growth.

The inability to subordinate self is the cornerstone of the micromanagement behaviors. In chapter 3, we will address the intense and frustrating behavior of the control and manipulation of time.

You Might Be Micromanaging If . . .

You really are not listening; you are just waiting to talk.

You say, "I told you so," or "It's not my fault," more than ten times a day.

You are perfectly willing to interfere with others but won't tolerate others interfering with you.

You have difficulty determining if the juice is really worth the squeeze.

Your favorite employees and peers remind you of yourself.

You don't have new problems and crises but recycle the same problems and crises over and over.

Your organization has a Hall of Fame, and you think your photo is the only one eligible to be displayed.

3

The Influence of Time

The control and manipulation of time are perhaps the most intense and frustrating of the micromanagement behaviors. People feel that their manager and peers rob them of control over their own time. Sixty-one percent of current managers and 59% of nonmanagers have experienced this behavior in the people to whom they report. Forty percent and 44%, respectively, have experienced it from peers, team members, or others. For many, the biggest impediment to doing their jobs well is the continual interruptions from their boss or others. "I don't have the time to do my job because someone always needs me to do something else" is a constant refrain in today's workplace.

The control and manipulation of time provokes reactions of intense resentment in top-quality performers and resigned complacency for others. People know that they will not be given enough time to do their job to the best of their ability, so they resign themselves to meeting only minimum standards of acceptability, and quality performers consistently feel overburdened. Micromanagement of time breeds negativity and mediocrity.

THE DICTATOR OF TIME

Micromanagers feel compelled to control the time allocations of others. This behavior results in people having constantly to create cover stories or embellished reports of how they have spent their time. The control and manipulation of time can invite dishonesty in others. One practitioner mandated that attendees at a professional association meeting should have "a minimum of twenty-five quality conversations with others, including ten in-depth conversations of twenty-five minutes or more." Can you just imagine people running around telling others, "If John asks, you tell him we talked for more than twenty-five minutes"?

✱ *Control and manipulation are not an interactive negotiation of time.*

They are not

> *What will you be working on today?*
>
> *How much time will you spend on this today?*
>
> *When can we get together on this?*

They are

> *I want you to work on this and only this today.*
>
> *This is exactly what I want you to do when you leave my office.*
>
> *Stop whatever you are doing and do this right now.*

The micromanager appears to lack confidence that others are capable of assessing their own workload and making good decisions on how their time should be allocated.

People's own perceptions of priority, project momentum, and creativity have little bearing on how their time should be invested. The only opinion of time and effort application that matters is that of the micromanager (another example of lack of subordination of self).

IMMEDIATE OBEDIENCE TO SUMMONS

Obviously, crises and problems do occur. Priorities and deadlines do shift. At times, it is necessary to shift attention away from one project or activity in favor of one that has increased in importance and intensity. However, micromanagers do not differentiate between legitimate situations and their impulses of the moment. People find themselves being pulled off projects and tasks in response to the micromanager's brain cramp of the moment. It sends the disrespectful message that "My stuff is important and your stuff is not."

In reality, the vast majority of a micromanager's interruptions are not "oxygen to dying people," although they are presented with that intensity. It is very difficult to understand true priorities when everything appears to be a 911 call.

People are not only frustrated by the interruptions; they resent the fact that they will ultimately be held accountable for the tasks they have been unable to complete because of today's "crisis." They begin to see the micromanager as unable to control his or her impulsive reactions, prone to panic, and void of any ability to prioritize tasks or exercise good judgment.

EXTREMELY HIGH VALUE PLACED ON THEIR OWN INDIVIDUAL TIME

Micromanagers continuously reinforce the implied messages that "My time is important and yours is not." They have no hesitation in interrupting people when they have a question or comment or even to share a self-perceived, amusing anecdote. They want to do it right now because it is a good time for them. Micromanagers are loathe to inquire

Is this a good time?

Should we get together later?

When would be a good time for you?

Yet micromanagers guard their own time very carefully. Office doors are closed, phone lines are parked on "do not disturb," and people are required to "make an appointment" or "get on my calendar" if they want to discuss something. They do not permit intrusions into their time. In a real crisis environment, few things are more frustrating than a cloistered manager or coworker who is unavailable or too busy to offer guidance, answer questions, or collaborate on grant approvals.

MISUSE/MISMANAGEMENT OF MEETINGS

Micromanager Debbie

Debbie is a regional manager for a Fortune 500 company in the defense industry. She is responsible for all regional quality and continuous improvement efforts. She manages a staff of fifteen people whose responsibilities include monitoring the internal quality efforts in both the manufacturing and administrative areas of the organization and working with suppliers to increase the quality of the products and service they provide.

Debbie expects her employees to be actively involved in the product and quality decisions of their suppliers. She wants them to train supplier personnel and, if necessary, influence supplier personnel decisions and promotions (activities that are highly resented by the supplier base).

Her staff is also responsible for providing quarterly updates to company executives, detailing quality improvements and dollar cost savings, and creating semiannual reports to their primary customer, the U.S. government. These reports include summaries for military leaders and purchasing officers concerning the company's efforts to improve quality, follow up on any previously identified areas of concern, and show cost savings yielded and passed along due to increased efficiency.

Within Debbie's region the company has four manufacturing plants (out of twelve nationwide), over thirty major and intermediate suppliers, and four military installations for which she and her continuous improvement staff are responsible.

The demands of the job require staff members to travel extensively within an eight-state region. According to plan, four members of the staff are required to spend 80% of their time traveling to company, supplier, and military locations. An additional six members of the staff are required to spend 60% of their time in similar travel. Five employees are based in the regional office with minimal travel requirements, functioning primarily in support roles.

Debbie is a "meeting freak." In fact, her under-the-radar nickname among her staff and with many others within the organization is "Yam" (yet another meeting). She requires a ninety-minute staff meeting at 8:30 A.M. every Monday morning (although staff members cannot recall a meeting that actually started or ended on time). The purposes of the Monday morning meetings are to establish expectations for the coming week, review any concerns, emphasize Debbie's priorities, and identify weekly plans for the internal support staff.

Routinely Debbie is involved in an earlier 8:00 A.M. meeting in another part of the building, which makes it relatively impossible for her to really begin her staff meeting by 8:30. Regardless of whether she is there or not, the entire staff is expected to assemble promptly and wait for her to start the meeting. No activity can begin in her absence, and woe be unto the person who isn't waiting patiently for the meeting to start upon her arrival. Debbie also allows interruptions that prolong the meetings. Staff members have tracked the number of times Debbie either is called out of their meetings or takes a cell phone call. (The mean is five times; the record is twelve.) By the time the meeting is finally concluded and the staff travels to their first site visit (which may be three states away), the entire day is wasted. This is a ninety-minute meeting with an eight- to ten-hour negative impact!

Debbie also requires a weekly summary meeting at 3:00 every Friday afternoon. The purposes of this meeting are to summarize the week's activities, identify potential problem areas of concern, and provide Debbie with ongoing data to meet her various reporting requirements.

She claims to require these meetings to ensure she is "kept up to speed" and "in the loop" on all activities. These meetings have never concluded before 5:30 (which really has a negative impact on morale, especially for those who have been away from home all week). Also, to make the 3:00 meeting, the traveling staff members frequently have to dedicate their entire Friday morning to getting back in time for the meeting. In a five-day work week, Debbie ties up two days with meetings and related travel. This limits some of her staff to 60% of their time to do their job!

Unfortunately, the meeting madness doesn't end there. Debbie frequently calls midweek "emergency," all-hands teleconference meetings. When notices of these meetings are sent out from the administrative staff, it usually reads something like this: "Yam has struck again. Thursday, 8:00 A.M., to discuss lack of relevant data concerning [something or other]."

While only a portion of the staff may actually have involvement with the issue of the moment, Debbie insists that everyone must be involved. All are required to participate in any midweek conference calls. Significant costs are incurred, critical amounts of productive time are wasted, and a drastic toll is taken on the potential for her group to be effective. At times these midweek meetings are deemed to be so important that she requires traveling people to head back to the office to attend in person.

Employees have developed some interesting behaviors in Debbie's meetings. They have learned not to raise questions or make any recommendations. They fear that her response would be "That's an excellent point. Let's schedule a meeting to pursue that further."

One field staff member said, "Debbie's meetings are agony. For Debbie, there is no horse too dead to beat."

Internal and external customers have often voiced frustration with the lack of availability of Debbie's staff. Field meetings are routinely cancelled because of Debbie's demands. Customers are annoyed because time commitments do not get met. Some suppliers are livid. One stated, "We are expected to jump through hoops to comply with their requirements just to keep their business, yet when we do, the quality representatives are not available to certify our compliance." Debbie's region has lost four quality improvement specialists in the last six months. Two key suppliers are reevaluating whether continuing to do business with Debbie's company is worth the "hassle."

The vice president of quality has approached Debbie with his concerns about customer complaints and the lagging productivity of her region.

Debbie can't figure out what to do to fix "her people." Duh.

Debbie is an example of at least four typical circumstances relating to micromanagers and meetings:

1. *Mismanagement of meeting time* Micromanagers will
   call a thirty-minute meeting and allow it to run for
   four hours! They have become gold medal performers in the art of taking ten minutes' worth of information and cramming it into a four-hour meeting.
   Apparently, they love the sound of their own voice.
   Those in attendance who have other activities or
   commitments planned for after the meeting have to
   reschedule or cancel, negatively impacting others
   who may be depending on them. Excessive time
   spent in meetings is time taken away from critical
   tasks and responsibilities. While meetings are a necessary part of workplace life, people resent their time
   being used unproductively.

   People who micromanage spend a significant
   amount of meeting time "telling" others what to do,
   discouraging questions and allowing discussion only
   in support of their position. They quickly choke off
   any comments that are interpreted as negative,
   oppositional, or resistant. Unfortunately, meetings
   are not used to expand knowledge or clarify priorities
   and tasks; they serve only to feed confusion and
   resentment.

2. *Requiring unnecessary meeting attendance* "All hands
   must be present for all meetings" is the micromanager's battle cry. Instead of involving only those

individuals to whom the meeting topic is relevant, everyone in the team/work group/department is required to attend. People who work with micromanagers invest an enormous amount of time sitting in meetings that have little or no relevance to them. To combat the boredom, they don't count sheep; they count how many times they say to themselves, "Why am I here?" Many people bring other work to do during the meeting, which provokes a negative response in micromanagers.

3. *Being late for meetings* Micromanagers are regularly late to their own meetings! Just like Debbie, they expect everyone else to be punctual, while not holding themselves to the same standard. Too frequently, people sit idle waiting for the person who called the meeting to show up and conduct the meeting. Besides being an enormous amount of wasted time and a staggering loss of productivity, the negative impact on morale and people's attitude is huge. Perhaps making people wait invokes a feeling of power and control in the micromanager, but it is very disrespectful, unproductive, and sends a message of extreme arrogance.

4. *Allowing distractions* Those who micromanage consistently allow themselves to be distracted during meetings, leaving others sitting and waiting while they focus on something else. (After all, their stuff is more important than your time.) Examples include

making or placing phone calls during meetings, encouraging others to call them out of meetings, and responding to a summons from higher up without dismissing the group. ("The vice president wants to meet with me. I'm sure this will be brief. Don't go anywhere. I'll be back as quickly as I can." Meanwhile, the meeting participants celebrate each other's *birthdays* waiting for the person's return.)

PERPETUATION OF CRISIS

Thriving on crisis, micromanagers are most happy when they can declare an emergency and really take over. Micromanagers pride themselves on being able to handle crisis situations. Crisis is the thief of time, eliminating opportunities for thoughtful discussion interaction and planning. Micromanagers revel in saying, "We are in a crisis here; we don't have time to discuss it—just do what I tell you to do."

Although many crisis situations are unavoidable, others are the result of the micromanager's crisis-creating behavior. Being submerged in day-to-day intricacies and minutia, micromanagers do not spend an appropriate amount of time in planning or prioritization. They focus so intently on today and the activity of the moment, they do not look at tomorrow or beyond. Consequently, the entire team/group/department is in a state of perpetual crisis. The micromanager's vision is at such a low range that problems, crises, or even extended deadlines approaching are not seen. When driving, if you only watch the road ten feet in front of your vehicle, you are consistently surprised by potholes, stop signs, and the brake lights of the cars in front of you. Normal driving situations become sudden occurrences, and urgent crisis responses are necessary.

People who work for and with micromanagers live in this perpetual crisis created by not looking forward. People exist in a pressure cooker of crisis and urgency, which robs them of the opportunity to do their jobs at a planful, performance-enhancing pace. Mediocre employees find this acceptable. It drives top-performing people up the wall!

DISTORTED DEADLINES

People who micromanage tend to impose unrealistic and sometimes unnecessary deadlines on others. If Friday would be an appropriate deadline, they insist that it must be done by Wednesday. Tight deadlines convey urgency and crisis. No consideration is extended to the person who is expected to meet the deadline. It is not "When can this be done?" It is "I must have this by. . . ."

If the deadline is artificial, the micromanager is probably not prepared to follow up when the task or project is delivered. (If the micromanager really does need it Friday, he or she will not act on it until Friday, so it sits for two days.)

Few things infuriate people more than being commanded to meet a pressure-packed deadline only to see their work languishing on someone else's desk. They quickly realize the "crisis" deadline was neither reasonable nor necessary. They learn to discount future microman-ager-imposed deadlines.

Here is a real-world example of peer-to-peer micro-management:

Andrew, an IT support rep, works in a fast-paced, pressure-packed environment. A significant percentage of his time is spent responding to internal technical problems within his organization. Nobody ever has "little" technical problems. Everyone thinks their problem is the most important thing on the planet and that it must be resolved right now. Andrew is very competent and enjoys his job, yet the constant mood of urgency and crisis does get to him. His internal customers judge him harshly when he cannot fix technical problems immediately. Andrew laments, "People do not understand technology, and they have no idea the time it takes to fix it."

Andrew's situation is further complicated by additional responsibilities. Andrew is required to assist one of his peers, Art, by participating in the design and testing of system mod-ifications. Andrew assists him in testing and writing formal evaluations and recommendations for potential system changes. Andrew generally enjoys this responsibility and welcomes the challenge of testing the work that is in progress. It also pro-vides variation in his duties. Unfortunately, sometimes these activities can be frustrating. Art consistently surprises him with the need to test something on the spur of the moment. Andrew feels like Art waits until he is in trouble before he asks for help. Art frequently panics and needs the formal written evaluation right now! Andrew knows he cannot do a good job of testing during the time available, even if there is nothing else to do. Obviously, he cannot stop responding to the normal service calls, so to do the testing he must come in hours before his normal starting time, work through lunch, and stay late. The problem is compounded because if people know he is in the building, they are continually calling him for service, whether he is supposed to be working or not. It is very difficult for him to dedicate the necessary amount of time to do the testing and evaluation thoroughly. Andrew says, "I really can't do the extensive testing that is necessary. I only have time to do some basic things. I don't do the more com-plex, time-consuming evaluation that can really identify and eliminate future problems. Because of this we have had some situations in the past where problems that should have been detected in testing became major heartburn later. I end up looking bad because I don't have the time to do the job right."

Andrew suspects that Art knows about these situations earlier and chooses not to ask for his help with enough time to allow him to do the work correctly. He blames Art's lack of planning. "Recently on a Friday afternoon, Art gave me a testing project and told me that he had to have the formal report by Tuesday. He acknowledged that the deadline was tight and knew that I would probably have to work on it over the weekend, but he insisted that he had to have the finished formal report on his desk by Tuesday. There was no room for negotiation. While I was working over the weekend, I real-

ized that Art wasn't even going to be back in the office until Thursday. The Tuesday deadline wasn't necessary, and I really didn't have to give up my personal time to get the project done. Yet Art was e-mailing and calling me continuously to make sure it was going to be done by Tuesday. This guy isn't even my boss, but he is driving me crazy."

When problems do occur with system modifications that could have been detected earlier if the appropriate time were given, Art blames Andrew. He tells their boss that any failure is because of Andrew's lack of support or poor testing efforts.

Would we be surprised that Andrew is contemplating getting an "Art Sucks" tattoo?

DISREGARD FOR PERSONAL CONSIDERATION

The personal considerations of others are unimportant to the micromanager. Any awareness of issues that may be important to others is subordinated to the micromanager's self-perceived urgent and important interests. The micromanager's message of "Do whatever you have to do to get this done—come in early, stay late, work through lunch," implies low value of anything but their requests. Their imposed work activities override any other requirements and totally disregard any personal considerations. Have you ever found yourself wanting to tell the micromanager to "get a life"?

Micromanagement Assessment

■ *Is the control and manipulation of time an issue?*

	Yes	No
1. Do you feel that it is important to influence or control how others spend their time?		
2. Do you believe that others consistently make good decisions on how to apply their time and effort?		
3. Do you escalate deadlines so that others will take your requests more seriously?		
4. Do you realize that your requests of others may be a significant disruption to their activities and responsibilities?		
5. Are you highly protective of your own time and resent the interruptions of others?		
6. Are you consistently available to others, avoiding any "do not disturb" messages or discouraging accessibility?		
7. Are meetings frequently delayed waiting for your appearance?		

	YES	No
8. When you are in charge of meetings, do you start on time and end on time?		
9. Do you perceive that you excel and feel comfortable in crises?		
10. Are you flexible in scheduling one-on-one conversations with others to avoid unnecessary interruptions for them?		
11. Are the majority of assignments you give to others or requests for help urgent and crisis driven?		
12. Do you believe that others see your requests as thoughtful and well planned?		

Any "yes" responses to the odd-numbered questions (1, 3, 5, 7, 9, 11) and "no" responses to the even-numbered questions (2, 4, 6, 8, 10, 12) indicate opportunities for self-evaluation and growth.

In chapter 4, we investigate the micromanagement behavior of controlling and dominating methodologies.

You Might Be Micromanaging If . . .

You hold three staff meetings weekly, including one on Friday at 4:00 P.M.

You are so task driven that you have no time for strategic planning and "big picture" thinking.

You don't have a life, and you resent people who do.

4

The Immortalization of Frank Sinatra
"My Way"

The title of this book, *My Way or the Highway,* is a phrase that is the essence of micromanagement. Five words that clearly capture the meaning of the micromanagement behavior of exercising relentless control over methodologies. People who micromanage attempt to rule and dominate "how" things are going to be done.

This behavior ranks number one on the micromanagement survey. Sixty-three percent of current managers and 71% of nonmanagers stated they have experienced this controlling behavior consistently from their managers. Thirty-seven percent of current managers and 42% of nonmanagers experience this behavior from peers, coworkers, and team members.

Confusion reigns when people do not understand the *W*s:

What is going to be done

Who is going to do it

Why it is necessary or important

When it must be completed

Where the activity will take place

If the *W*s are clarified, along with a clear awareness of the policies, procedures, mission, vision, and rules of the road, people can usually figure out *how* to do something. Whenever possible, individuals or work groups should be engaged in discussions and decisions of *how* tasks, goals, objectives, and responsibilities will be achieved. The people with daily exposure to the issue and challenges must have control over the methodologies used to accomplish them. This is a concept that micromanagers just do not seem to comprehend.

The strategies of empowerment and participation have, at their roots, the willingness to allow others to influence methodology. As long as policies and procedures are followed, and the requirements of time, budget, and quality are met, and they stay between the white lines to accomplish the *how*, the lane they choose to drive in is relatively unimportant. Involving others in discussions and decisions of methodology or how things can be done gives them a stake in successful outcomes. What is impacted is *who* gets the credit or recognition for success. The inability to subordinate self makes it very difficult for some people to give away any control over methodologies and outcomes because they want total control and total recognition.

The control and domination of methodology is frustrating to others and counterproductive to quality and efficiency. Micromanagers impose methods on others that may be less productive, less comfortable, and counterintuitive and then perceive that they must watch them closely to make sure that they do it right! The micromanager's perception that "You can't trust other people to do it right" translates to "If I don't watch them closely, they will do it their own way and not mine."

In today's collaborative work environment, we are bombarded with messages that people should be encouraged to

- "buy in" to all initiatives,
- be "engaged" in decision making,
- take "ownership" of their jobs, and
- "wrap their arms around" what they do.

The best way to accomplish these euphemisms is by letting people determine their own way of getting things done. Give people some measure of control, especially in areas of their greatest level of expertise, and the yield will be enhanced outcomes. People tend to excel at that which they help create. Tell them how to do it, and they resent you. Give them the information and let them figure it out, and they work hard to prove themselves right. Unfortunately, those who micromanage just do not seem to get it!

RESPONSIBILITY FOR HAVING
THE RIGHT ANSWER

Micromanagers generate the perception that they have all the answers. They dismiss the intellect, experience, knowledge, and training of the people around them in favor of promoting their own. This invalidates the input of others and puts an enormous amount of pressure on the micromanager. They are expected to always have the right answer. No one (regardless of what micromanagers may think about themselves) is that bright. The collective intellect is often silenced by the singular intellect of one. Great strength is contained in the phrase "I am not sure I know the best way to do this. *How* do you think it should be done?" Micromanagers perceive this statement as weakness.

HIERARCHICAL DUMBNESS

In organizations where the culture of micromanagement is pervasive, there is an overall assumption that the higher you are in the organization, the higher your IQ. Intellect dwindles as you go down through the organization. The people at the top are assumed to be the only ones who can think and have all the right answers.

People who micromanage project the arrogant message of "Me smart—you stupid." They will tell you how to do everything.

I recently experienced an unfortunate example of hierarchical dumbness.

I was invited to be the keynote speaker at the annual awards dinner for an electronic manufacturing organization. Various people were being honored for their achievements during the past fiscal year, and the last person honored was a gentleman named Joe who was retiring from the company after thirty years of service. Joe was thanked for his years of dedicated service and was given some retirement gifts. As Joe was walking away from the head table, some people in the audience clamored for him to say a few words. (Eating utensils were banged on water glasses and people started shouting, "Speech, speech, speech!") Joe was mortified. He was not accustomed to speaking in public, and he had prepared no remarks. He wasn't expecting this. If he could have kept walking, he would have been fine. Unfortunately for Joe, he froze and the president gestured for him to step back up to the microphone. When the crowd quieted down, and after a pause that seemed like an eternity, Joe, with tears in his eyes, looked at the president and said, "For thirty years you paid for my hands. I would have given you my brain for free if only you would have asked."

Joe was not a highly educated man, but he did have a brain. He had been a loyal contributor as an hourly worker in the manufacturing area for thirty years. He did possess a wealth of knowledge and experience. He undoubtedly had some answers to problems and ideas that would have been worth considering. It was truly a shame that on the big night of his retirement, his parting thoughts were sadness and resentment that he had never been asked to help in any way. He could have helped determine how to do things more efficiently.

As a keynote speaker, that was a tough act to follow! Joe certainly took the air out of the room, as most everyone nodded and murmured in agreement. The audience could identify with what he was saying.

It is particularly frustrating to people when they are apparently expected to park their brains at the door and let somebody else do their thinking for them. Resentment runs high when input into methodologies is low. There is a direct correlation between the influence over how things will be done and overall employee morale. If influence is low, morale plummets.

The following example of micromanagement provided the basis for naming both this chapter and this book.

Micromanager Frances

Frances was the director of purchasing for a major university in the Southwest. She had a staff of seven professional purchasing agents, ten administrative support people, two financial specialists, and one technology person. Frances had been known to rule her domain with an iron fist. Her staff had nicknamed her "Frankie" as in the female version of Frank Sinatra. The basis for this nickname was her penchant for

always insisting on doing things "my way." If the phrase
"my way or the highway" ever applied to anyone, it undoubt-
edly did to Frances.

Her entire staff agreed that it was futile to offer ideas or
suggestions concerning their work. It was always "do it the
way Francis wants it done—period." The staff learned very
quickly not to exercise initiatives or take risk. They basically
would wait to be told how to do everything that Frances
assigned. The purchasing staff considered themselves to be
in a "brain-free, no-thinking zone."

One person lamented, "No one makes decisions around
here. We just wait for Frances to rule on everything." There is
never a consideration of the best way of doing something,
only figuring out how Frances would handle it and do it that
way. If something was done differently than she would com-
mand, she made life miserable.

When Frances announced her retirement, there was great
joy within her staff. While a retirement party was held on
her final workday, the real party began the Monday after she
left. The staff met that Monday evening at a local tavern/
restaurant for their own celebration of joy. A few of the sup-
port staff banded together to write the following song that
was sung (badly) to the tune of Frank Sinatra's "My Way":

And now the end is here
And we celebrate her retirement
And friends we say it clear
She was the queen of micromanagement.

Her control was intense and full
It was always her way or the highway.
Our jobs were no more than this
To just do it her way.

Complaints, we had more than a few
But we would never, dare to mention
We did what we had to do.
It was her way, without exemption

She planned everything we did
It was her way or the highway
And regardless of what you thought
She said, "Do it my way."

Yes, there were times when we all knew
She bit off more than she could chew.
But through it all, she had no doubt
If you complained, then you were out.
She faced it all and stood so tall
While we did it her way.

Together, we've laughed and cried
We've had our fill of her abusing.
Our joy will not subside
And we find it all so amusing
To think we did all that
And may we say, not in a shy way,
It was never about any of us
We all did it her way.

For who is Frankie, what has she got
If not herself, then she has naught.
She said the things she truly feels
And we were the ones who always kneeled.
The record shows we took the blows
And we did it her way.

Would you want that to be the legacy you left behind?

TIME AND PRESSURE

The trend of micromanagers justifying their behavior because of time constraints, deadlines, and overall performance pressures is obvious. Instead of taking the time to involve others in discussions and decisions of *how* things can be done, they perceive it to be easier, more expedient, and time-efficient simply to just tell people *how* to do it. It is, in fact, more "comfortable" for micromanagers. In times of crisis, it is usually necessary to control and impose how things are done. As we have discussed, people who micromanage love to perpetuate crisis and exercise control over *how*.

REJECTION OF EXTERNAL INFLUENCE

A main component of micromanagers' inflexibility is the perception that somehow it is "different" for them in their area of influence. Their situation is "different"; the people they work with are "different"; their processes are "different." Plans and strategies that have worked well for others won't work for them because the situation and circumstances are "different." Micromanagers frequently feel that the people around them are just not ready for either advanced techniques or decision making. Not surprisingly, the micromanager believes that he or she is the only one who has enough special knowledge to recognize the "difference." Because of this, the micromanager rejects ideas, models, and methods that are not homegrown (initiated by the micromanager).

One example of this situation is the rejection of best practice learning.

Discovering best practices is a very relevant and effective technique used in organizational training and development. By definition, *best practice* is discovering how another individual or organization dealt with a circumstance similar to yours. It is finding out *how* others have achieved success. There certainly is no guarantee that the strategies, techniques, and tactics that work for others will automatically work for you or your organization. However, there is no guaranteed certainty that they will not work, either. Success can be enhanced, problems solved, and efficiencies increased by discovering strategies that have been proven to work. Learning from best practices helps

- avoid reinventing the wheel,
- learn from the mistakes of others,

- benefit from tested methods, and

- expand the base of knowledge and options.

Unfortunately, micromanagers frequently deny themselves the opportunity to learn from the experiences of others. They predetermine incompatibility, irrelevance, and situational variation.

It won't work here. We're different.

What worked for that team won't work for ours.

That may have worked for you, but it certainly won't work for us.

What worked for an organization in New York or California won't work for us here.

Once again, micromanagers impose on themselves the limitations of their own vision, intellect, and experience by being unwilling or unable to incorporate the vision, intellect, and experience of others.

NEGATION OF TRAINING

A particularly devastating example of how micromanagers attempt to control and dominate methodology is the negation of training. Most employees look forward to training and development, welcoming the opportunity to increase their inventory of skills, raise their value, and position themselves for growth and mobility. Many (not all) organizations invest a great deal of time, resources, and expense in training employees. People who micromanage tend to dismiss what other people have learned; after all, "things are different" for them and their area of responsibility. They want things done "my way," not the way the training department wants, not according to best practices or standard work requirements. Their way is the only way.

Do any of these phrases sound familiar?

I don't care what you learned in training. Here's how we do it in my area.

The training the company provides is all well and good, but we do it differently here.

The classroom stuff that they teach really doesn't apply here in the real world. We do it differently.

All the investment of time, resources, and expense is wasted because people who micromanage insist on using their own methodologies and what they know best. The people who are trained experience terribly high frustration and resentment because their time and effort have been wasted. They are not given the opportunity to implement the things they have learned. They are not permitted to practice their new skills. Even if they have the opportunity to use those skills later in their career, it is difficult or impossible to maintain proficiency in skills that are not practiced and reinforced on a regular basis.

Sometimes the negation of training has tragic consequences, as the next example illustrates.

John sued his employer for an injury he suffered on the job. He received significant damage to his right hand and forearm when it was caught in the machinery he operated as part of his job as a production technician.

The company denied John compensation, alleging that he did not follow safety procedures. He failed to use the safety guard that is required each time the equipment is used. They claimed that John was given extensive training on safety procedures when he was hired by the company, which he failed to follow.

In his court testimony, John acknowledged that he had, in fact, been trained to use the safety device properly. He also testified that when his training was completed and he reported to work on his shift, Steve, the foreman who was his immediate supervisor, told him, "I don't care what they taught you in training class. In this department on my shift, the safety guard isn't necessary. It's just overkill—too much of a precaution. The machine is safe. Besides that, we don't want to take the time securing and removing the safety device each time we run the machine. It just wastes time that kills our productivity. We have to make our numbers, and if we don't, we are all in trouble. We can't afford to slow the process down by using unnecessary safety equipment. That's not how we do it in my area."

Seven other employees who were hired at the same time as John testified that Steve gave them the same instructions. They also confirmed that Steve criticized them if their speed in the process was slowed down by using the safety device

properly. It was clearly established that not using the safety
device was standard operating procedure for Steve's employ-
ees. Whether the company was aware of Steve's deviation
from the safety policy was unclear; however, it was clear
that Steve was regarded as the top supervisor in productivity
ratings.

Employees from other shifts testified that they were
trained to use the safety device and encouraged to do so by
their foreman. They also testified that they experienced no
significant reduction in the efficiency of their process and no
loss time injuries.

John won his lawsuit. Negation of training extracted a
painfully high price.

THE NEGATIVE IMPACT OF CONTROL AND DOMINATION OF METHODOLOGIES

In general, methodologies erode over time. The negative
impact is not immediate, but it becomes more deeply en-
trenched the longer it continues. The most intense results
of this behavior are as follows:

- **Resentment** People react very negatively to always
  being told *how* they have to do something. Anger
  and a perception of being seen as stupid or incom-
  petent escalate. People feel they are being treated like
  children.

- **Extinguished initiative** The control and domination of methodology over an extended period of time tends to induce a comalike state in others.

- **Abandonment** Many people, especially top performers, will seek greener pastures where they will be permitted to think and perform to their optimum ability. Turnover and retention become significant issues.

- **Obsolescence: personal and group** The rut of consistent methodology has been described as the equivalent of a coffin with the ends kicked out. There is no growth; there is no development either for the individual or the group as a whole. This frequently results in downsizing, contracting out, or job loss.

- **Creating the "disloyal opposition"** The more input into methodology is denied, the more some people will begin actually to work against micromanagers, either overtly or covertly. Some become committed to ensuring that micromanagers are wrong, working to prove that the mandated ways do not work. As you will see in Part III, this negative impact can be reversed if the appropriate corrective action is implemented.

As we move to chapter 5, we address the micromanagement behaviors of requiring excessive approvals. This is especially problematic because it impacts both people and process and contributes to micromanagers becoming bottlenecks.

Micromanagement Assessment

■ *Is dominating methodology an issue?*

	YES	NO
1. Have you successfully adapted externally influenced changes in the last twelve months?		
2. Do you feel that others would be more successful by consistently doing things your way?		
3. Do you consistently communicate the what, why, when, and let others determine the how?		
4. Do people enthusiastically engage your ideas without significant resistance?		
5. Do some people seem to want your ideas to fail?		
6. Do other people's knowledge and experience bring creativity and innovation to methodology discussions?		
7. Do crisis situations provide opportunities for others to contribute ideas?		

	Yes	No
8. Do you always expect yourself to have the right answer?		
9. Are the best practice experiences of others relevant to your situation?		
10. Are the internal and external training opportunities available to you and others relevant to your real-world situation?		
11. Are the people in your environment, especially those you influence, significantly different from people in other areas or organizations?		
12. Is there any relationship between how methodologies are determined and issues of morale, retention, and productivity in your area of influence?		

Any "no" responses to questions 1, 3, 4, 6 7, 9, 10, and 12 and "yes" responses to questions 2, 5, 8, and 11 indicate opportunities for self-evaluation and growth.

You Might Be Micromanaging If . . .

Someone asks, "How should this be done?" and your response is "My way."

You think your IQ jumped twenty points just because you got promoted or you are in charge of something.

The only best practices that matter are your own.

5

■   ■   ■

Approval
Requirements

If we developed a caricature of a micromanager, it would
be the neck of a bottle with a face on it. Bottlenecks are
created by micromanagers. They become a funnel with
everything moving through them.

Picture a highway system with eight or ten lanes sud-
denly narrowing into only one lane for a toll booth. All lanes
feed into one lane where vehicles stop for a transaction to
occur. Forward progress is halted and then begins again
slowly as vehicles pass through the toll booth. It takes a
while to regain speed and momentum. Micromanagers are
that toll booth. The transaction is their required approval.

Most state or local highway departments have developed a computerized system to allow vehicles that travel
through toll areas frequently to do so with little or no hindrance to their progress. Prepurchased stickers are displayed
and read by computers as the vehicle passes through the
toll area. Micromanagers can learn an awful lot from this
analogy.

In the micromanagement survey, 56% of current managers and 63% of nonmanagers have experienced this behavior from their managers. The number for peers, team members, and coworkers is much lower: 25% for current managers and 23%for nonmanagers. Usually the necessity for seeking approvals from peers, team members, and coworkers is not required; however, they can become bottlenecks as well.

THE DISTORTION OF RESPONSIBILITY AND AUTHORITY

For most micromanagers, the term *empowerment* means the sharing of responsibility with others, but not the sharing of authority. They exercise control by requiring that others receive their approval for decisions, changes, and courses of action. No one goes forward without their blessing. This is a major contributor to the high stress levels in today's work environment. Micromanagers are the Typhoid Mary's of stress and burnout!

In the perfect world of micromanagers, everyone else is held accountable for the responsibilities over which the micromanager maintains authority. They work hard to create their version of heaven, while creating pockets of hell for those around them.

Have you ever heard statements like these from a micromanager?

You're responsible for this—but before you do anything with it, check with me.

You're responsible for this—but don't make any changes without my approval.

You're responsible for this—but clear it with me before you make any decisions.

THE PERCEPTIONS OF LOW VALUE
OF OTHERS

A common theme throughout our discussion is the perceived low value of others. Micromanagers assume that others are somehow less than equal to them, and they demonstrate a lack of trust in others' skills and abilities. Whether this message is intentional or not, it has a devastating impact on morale, motivation, and self-esteem. Micromanagers do not empower or promote decision making in others. If people are treated as incompetents, they will behave as incompetents.

TODAY'S ACCELERATED TIME DEMANDS

The accelerated pace of today's workplace does not permit micromanagers the luxury of requiring people to pause in their productivity to secure unnecessary approvals. Every time an individual's actions or decisions must be approved by someone else, a loss of time and productivity occurs.

Minutes add up to hours. Certainly, there are times when approvals are necessary; however, serious evaluation must be done to guarantee that approvals truly add value to the process. Is an approval necessary to ensure quality or compliance? (Or is it only to increase the micromanager's control over people or process?) What are we protecting ourselves or our organization from by not allowing people to take action and make decisions?

MICROMANAGEMENT AND LOST OPPORTUNITY

In today's fast-paced business environment, prompt action frequently provides advantages over the competition. Quick response maximizes these opportunities. In the absence of a quick response, because of a micromanager's approval requirements, these advantages are minimized or lost.

THE BURDEN OF AVAILABILITY/ ACCESSIBILITY

When micromanagers demand that their approval is required before any "go forward" action can be taken, they place a terrible burden on themselves. They must be available and on call at all times. When micromanagers are unavailable or inaccessible, activities grind to a screeching halt. Individuals and organizations suffer when micromanagers are on vacation, attend meetings, or are out sick. This is a good news/bad news thing. The good news is, when micromanagers are unavailable, they are not around to interfere with what people do; the bad news is, when micromanagers are not around to give approval, little to nothing can get done.

If one of the true tests of personal efficiency is how well things run in your absence, micromanagers flunk that test.

Micromanager Vance

Vance accepted a position as the HR director of a medical equipment manufacturing plant. The plant had approximately three thousand unionized hourly employees and six hundred salaried management and staff people. Vance replaced an HR director who was perceived by the senior executive management team to be soft and inconsistent in dealing with the union. Vance was appointed to ensure that organizational policies and procedures, including the existing collective bargaining agreement, were adhered to consistently. He was charged with eliminating any and all failures to enforce the existing rules. In other words, Vance was brought in to kick butt!

One of the first changes Vance made was a requirement that he be personally consulted in every circumstance where disciplinary action could be involved. If an employee was to be disciplined for absenteeism, tardiness, safety violations, or some other offense, he must preapprove the discipline. In his attempt to stop employees from flaunting the rules and regulations, he was insisting that more controls be implemented. In short, Vance's preapproval was required in all matters.

This situation created a huge frustration to the supervisors and managers. Because of the requirement of contacting Vance with each occurrence, there was a great loss of time and productivity while tracking him down and awaiting his decision. The union leadership was also frustrated. Vance was making decisions after hearing only one side of the story. The union's position was ignored.

The plant was on a twenty-four-hour manufacturing cycle, so Vance was receiving calls day and night. His beeper was constantly erupting, resulting in disruption to his family and personal life. Important meetings had to be interrupted so that Vance could excuse himself and respond to the summons of his beeper. It was not uncommon for a supervisor and his or her manager, the employee in question, and a union representative to be standing around waiting for Vance to respond.

Instead of clarifying the level of authority that supervisors and managers could exercise in dealing with discipline problems, and instructing them in the criteria for making consistent decisions, Vance held all authority himself. Because he was the only one who clearly understood the decision-making criteria, not only was he the only one who could make them, but his decisions often appeared to be inconsistent, capricious, and arbitrary.

A further complication arose in Vance's micromanagement behavior. This one actually had legal implications concerning the union contract, which contained a four-step grievance process:

Step 1: *When a grievance was filed, the union steward
and the supervisor or manager involved were to address
the situation as soon as possible and make every attempt
to resolve it in a timely manner. (Vance's policy of
approval obviously forbade this from happening in any
cases involving discipline.)*

Step 2: *If the grievance could not be addressed in step 1,
then a higher-ranking chief shop steward and the next
midlevel manager (production or quality manager) were
to review the unresolved grievance within five working
days in an attempt to achieve resolution.*

Step 3: *If the grievance was still unresolved, senior
union leadership (president or vice president) and a
representative of senior plant management were to meet
with the HR director for an "unbiased" ruling. The HR
director was intended to be an "impartial" third party
who served as the bridge between the union and management. The HR director would then issue a ruling
resolving the grievance.*

*The HR director (Vance), who was supposed to be the
impartial third party in step 3, was actually the same
person who approved the disciplinary action in step 1.
Vance was in a position of reviewing and affirming the
action that required his approval in the first place! He
was approving his own work. Needless to say, he did not
rule against himself. The union did not win too many
step 3 grievance appeals.*

*This situation was the equivalent of receiving a
speeding ticket, going to court to contest it, and finding*

that the judge and jury are the same officer who wrote the ticket in the first place!

Step 4: *If the ruling of the HR director was unacceptable either to management or the union, either side could file for external arbitration. This is a very costly process. It involves hiring attorneys or an external arbitration person. Both sides professed the desire to avoid arbitration at all costs and save the drain on dollars and time.*

When the senior vice president of human resources became aware of the inefficiency and unfairness of Vance's micromanaged process, she made significant adjustments. Policies were put in place ensuring that all HR directors and employees involved in the HR function were expressly forbidden from being involved in day-to-day decisions that could result in discipline or grievances. It was mandated that authority be returned to the floor supervisors and managers. Training was provided concerning corporate policies and the existing contractual agreement to ensure consistent decision making.

A CONVENIENT TARGET FOR BLAME

Many micromanagers do not realize that their behavior of requiring others to seek excessive approval makes them an easy target for blame. They self-create an inviting donkey on which others can pin the tail of negative responsibility. It is easy and tempting for others to defend their lack of progress or success because of the micromanager's demand for approval.

It's not my fault—I can't make those decisions.

I could not move forward because I needed her approval.

I was stuck and couldn't take action until I was able to find him.

What was I supposed to do? I didn't have the authority to go any further.

People who are not given decision-making authority may do everything within their power to insulate themselves from negative accountability at the expense of the one holding the authority. This can have a devastating impact on the careers of people who micromanage.

THE TRAP OF SELF-PERCEIVED INDISPENSABILITY

People who micromanage appear to be driven to make themselves indispensable. They want to create situations where the organization or the process will not work without them. It is not how good they make others or the growth and development of the people around them that matters; what matters most is that they position themselves to be the linchpin that holds everything together.

One of the primary methods of reinforcing their indispensability is requiring their input or approval consistently throughout a process. The reality is, micromanagers are not nearly as indispensable as they would like to think. It is self-deception at its finest. Most organizations have become painfully aware that being dependent on any one individual is a very vulnerable situation. Effective organizations move quickly to dilute the indispensability. Requiring excessive approvals increases risk and vulnerability, not indispensability.

INAPPROPRIATE EXTENDED ORGANIZATIONAL INFLUENCE

Some micromanagers actually use their demands for approvals as a tactic to gain greater influence at the expense of others. While micromanagers may see this as their advantage, it can have a crippling effect on others, perhaps even the entire organization. The negative result of this behavior can even impact customers, clients, and others externally.

Here is an example.

A public school system was undertaking a major upgrade of its technology system. A local benefactor was contributing in excess of $5.5 million to purchase laptop computers for students in the seventh through twelfth grades and to upgrade the entire school system's internal technology capabilities.

Implementing the upgrade was a major challenge. Buildings would have to be rewired, the technology curriculum would have to be changed to teach students how to use their new laptops, and it would be necessary to adopt consistent software programs to be used throughout the system (a welcome change for all).

The superintendent of schools created a technology response committee to support the adaptation of the systemwide changes.

The committee consisted of principals and facility directors from all of the schools within the system (fifteen buildings in all), individual representatives from the technology department representing the system's intranet and hardware capabilities, the faculty member who chaired the computer development department, the systems curriculum director (an assistant superintendent), and a representative of the parent–teacher organization.

The committee was given a substantial budget and had authority to make any and all decisions that were necessary. It was their job to get it all done.

Micromanager Cameron

Cameron was in charge of curriculum development for the school system. Because of her busy calendar and various responsibilities, she was unable to attend many of the technology response committee meetings and work sessions. She designated one of her assistants, Paul, to attend the meetings in her absence. Paul was given the responsibility of submitting reports and data from Cameron and participating in all of the discussions pertinent to the adaptation of the new technology system. Paul, however, was not given the authority to participate in making any actual decisions. Everyone else who attended the meetings had the authority to vote yes or no on decisions except for Paul. When decisions were being considered, Paul's consistent response was "Let me take this information back to Cameron so that she can make her decision." This approach obviously interfered with the entire committee's ability to make decisions. It was espe-cially problematic in situations that demanded an immediate response. This method allowed Cameron to have the ability to execute a death sentence on all committee decisions. Instead of being a part of the collaborative work and deci-sion-making process, she was in a position to approve or disapprove activities and decisions after the fact. The com-mittee did the heavy lifting while Cameron sat back and exercised significant control. The committee was intended to be a group of equals, but Cameron's behavior allowed her to become the unintended, dominant, and controlling member of the group.

Not only was this situation frustrating to the other committee members, but it was not in the school system's best interest. Issues of primary interest to Cameron were given much greater weight than those of other important areas. One result was that a standardized internal operating and software system was never adopted (which was not really important to Cameron). This micromanagement behavior added both time and expense to the project.

Unfortunately, the committee was unable to counter Cameron's influence, and the outcome was very different from what was originally intended. Resentment by some leaders within the school system resulted, as well as political opposition within the community to the final outcome.

The benefactor was ultimately unhappy with how the gift was utilized and indicated a reluctance to comply with future, previously committed donations. Cameron's micromanagement behaviors did pervasive damage beyond what her position and participation should have allowed.

MICROMANAGERS' DEFENSE OF THEIR GOOD JUDGMENT

Micromanagers defend their behavior of requiring approvals by insisting that their only motivation is to ensure that good judgment and common sense are exercised. They also want to "protect" employees from making mistakes and guard against impulsive or unwise decisions.

The problem lies in the micromanagers' definition of good judgment and common sense. They see it through their own eyes. People exercise good judgment, use common sense, and do the right thing when they do exactly what the micromanagers would do. If micromanagers agree, then the decision is sound. If they disagree, then it is a flawed decision. If their goal is to ensure consistency in decisions, application of rules, and policies/procedures, then everyone must clearly understand the decision-making criteria. When people understand it, they are usually capable of making their own high-quality decisions.

THE NEGATIVE IMPACT OF EXCESSIVE DEMANDS FOR APPROVAL

The impact of this behavior occurs immediately. The interference with people and the process involved is significant. If there is a gradual increase in the excessive demand for approvals, there is a corresponding decrease in productivity and efficiency. The negative impact continues until appropriate corrections are made.

Extinguished Risk Taking

Micromanagement behaviors teach people not to take risks or show initiative. When the micromanager makes it obvious that people are not savvy enough to make decisions and must be protected against making mistakes, they quickly become unwilling to step up with their ideas. Creativity, exercising initiative, and the appropriate taking of risk are common casualties when excessive demands for approvals are required. When people are needed to create, initiate, or think on their feet, they are less prepared or willing to take the risk.

Failure to Develop Others and Prepare Them
to Take Over the Micromanager's Job

In the quest to make themselves indispensable, microman-agers frequently anchor themselves in concrete. If no one else can make the decisions, if people are not capable of acting without approval, not only will they never move up in the organization, but neither will the micromanager. This is a classic lose/lose.

✱ *People who micromanage appear to be threatened by the growth and development of others, when in fact, they should be supporting it if for no other reason than their own personal gain. If no one is capable of replacing you, how will you get promoted?*

Crisis Unpreparedness

When authority and approvals are centralized in someone who micromanages, it is extremely difficult for anyone else to step up in a crisis situation. If no one else knows why certain decisions are made or what should be done next, no one is prepared to act in the micromanager's absence. If the micromanager goes away, his or her unshared reservoir of decision-making criteria goes, too.

Potential for Abuse

The potential for abuse escalates when there is no balance and when authority is not shared. This is not to say that all who demonstrate this micromanagement behavior are dishonest or will become abusive. Most are just trying to do their job as they know how to do it. However, if all authority is funneled to one person and others are dependent on approvals, the potential for unhealthy, unethical, and illegal circumstances to develop is very real.

Customers Pay a Price

Processes that are encumbered by excessive demands for approvals ultimately impact customers. They feel the impact when the organization is not flexible enough to react with timeliness and decisiveness to changing needs and market fluctuations. If your organization cannot respond quickly to their needs, customers will find others that can. Slowness in response is a quick step into irrelevance and obsolescence.

Cost of Underutilization

It is an expensive waste of resources when capable people are paid for doing less than they are trained and hired to do. If you are not going to let people think, make decisions, and exercise some measure of control over their environment, why are you paying them so much?

If you hire the best and brightest, demanding excessive approvals does not allow them to be the best and brightest.

Micromanagement Assessment

■ *Are excessive approval requirements an issue?*

	YES	No
1. Are you ever accused of being a bottleneck?		
2. Do you require people to seek your approval to ensure that you don't lose control?		
3. Do people consistently have the authority to follow up on your requests?		
4. Are others ever hindered in moving forward waiting for you to approve their progress or next step?		
5. Do you believe that the process cannot be streamlined to reduce the number of approvals that are necessary?		
6. Have you recently increased anyone's decision-making authority?		
7. Do you consider others to have made a good decision and exercised common sense when they do exactly what you would have done?		
8. Do you perceive that you could personally accomplish much more if you didn't have to review and approve other people's work?		

	YES	No
9. Do others have a clear understanding of your decision-making criteria?		
10. Do you feel constrained or infringed upon because of having to be available or accessible to others?		
11. Are you a frequent target for blame?		
12. Do the people around you take appropriate risk and exercise initiative?		

"No" responses to questions 3, 6, 9, and 12 and "yes" responses to the other questions (1, 2, 4, 5, 7, 8, 10, 11) indicate opportunities for self-evaluation.

You Might Be Micromanaging If . . .

You have overruled someone else's choice on where to have their birthday luncheon.

You resent your cell phone and pager always going off when you are the one requiring people to get your approval.

You have ever initiated or received work-related phone calls in your bathtub.

You have to approve every office supply requisition, and you rejected an order for twelve pencils because you only have eleven people in the office.

6

■ ■ ■

Dysfunctional Monitoring and Reporting

M onitoring and reporting are legitimate organizational requirements. Here are some typically monitored events:

- Activities

- Progress on tasks and projects

- Compliance with regulations, policies, protocols, and laws

- Process improvement

- Attention to priorities

- Timelines in meeting deadlines

"Find the flaw and fix it early" is a phrase that captures the essence of effective monitoring.

Reporting is the preestablished requirement to formally present specific data, summaries of activity, and results of

117

predetermined indicators. Most reporting has agreed-on deadlines for submission and may be in writing or delivered face-to-face. In micromanaged environments, people are required to write reports that they know nobody reads!

In the micromanagement survey, 53% of current managers and 52% of nonmanagers have experienced what they perceive to be dysfunctional monitoring and reporting requirements from their managers. Twenty-five percent of both groups have experienced it from peers, team members, and coworkers.

Traditionally, monitoring was viewed as a management responsibility, and reporting was a requirement imposed throughout in the organization. In today's workplace, we all have 360-degree responsibilities for monitoring and reporting. In our collaborative work environments, it becomes increasingly necessary for us to keep peers, customers, and managers informed of our activities and progress.

The dysfunctional use of these tools can quickly become micromanagement. People who micromanage misuse these tools to stifle, suffocate, and frustrate the people around them. A number of years ago, the term *MBWA* (management by walking around) was coined and used as an effective, informal, nonthreatening way of monitoring activities and progress. Micromanagers have invented *MBBSS* (management by becoming second skin). The difference between MBWA and MBBSS is equivalent to the difference between a butterfly and a leech.

The micromanager's use of monitoring and reporting is focused on three priorities:

Prove to me that you have been busy.

Prove to me that you are doing what I think is important.

Prove to me that you are doing it my way.

The overuse of monitoring and reporting is an extension of the micromanager's compulsion to always be present. They are driven to stay on top of things and always know what is going on. Several key factors are involved in this dysfunctional monitoring and reporting behavior.

INABILITY OR UNWILLINGNESS TO ESTABLISH AND COMMUNICATE EXPECTATIONS

As previously mentioned, people who micromanage are inconsistent in identifying clear, concise expectations. They are not exactly sure of what they want, but they are confident that they will know "it" when they see it. Because of this, they have to see "it" frequently to know whether or not it is acceptable. They want to see "it" at every step of the way to be sure "it" looks like what they want. They want to know immediately if "it" starts to look different.

All too often, the vision of what they want exists solely in their eyes. They can tell you what is wrong, but they cannot tell you what you can do to improve it or make it right. Micromanagers feel compelled to check on progress continuously to ensure that their illusive standards of acceptability are being met. Trying to meet the expectations of a micromanager deteriorates into a guessing game.

THE MICROMANAGER AS "CRITICAL PARENT"

Micromanagers have much in common with a parent who, when his child comes home with five A's and one B on her report card, immediately criticizes the B. The outstanding effort, the A grades, are ignored. The less than perfect effort becomes the focus. While it may be appropriate to be concerned about a brilliant student's B, the exceptional performance should be recognized and praised. Unfortunately, the critical parent and micromanager only emphasize the negative. The good is taken for granted.

MONITORING THE WRONG THINGS

Micromanagers often monitor the wrong things or monitor the right things wrongly. People who micromanage have selective critical evaluation patterns. They look at certain elements of performance and productivity too closely and become very "micro" in their observations. To them, monitoring equals "microscoping."

Being Blinded by Activity

Micromanagers appear to value the illusion of activity over the reality of effectiveness. This is the basis for much of the "prove to me that you have been busy" focus of their monitoring and reporting activity.

There is a huge difference between being busy and being effective. People who come in fifteen minutes early and stay fifteen minutes late yet do not get a lot accomplished are favored over individuals who are very productive and arrive and leave on time. Those who overschedule meetings and are always running from one commitment to another and are so busy that they cannot get their work done on time are preferred over people who know how to say no and consistently meet their deadlines. If you are calm and in control, the micromanager thinks you do not have enough to do. If you are harried, overstressed, and near a meltdown, your pace is just about right.

Derek graduated with his MBA and joined a Fortune 500 organization as a senior budget analyst. He was excited about his new job and full of confidence that this position was a mere stepping stone to future organizational greatness. One of the first things Derek did when starting his new assignment was to analyze the behavior patterns of his new boss. He knew what kind of car the boss drove, where he parked, when he arrived each day, and when he went home. Derek committed himself to making sure he arrived ten minutes before the boss each day and never left work until the boss was gone. Apparently, Derek assumed that his boss placed a high value on the illusion of activity.

On Friday, at the end of his fourth week on the job, Derek became frustrated because the boss was not leaving on time. He kept checking the parking lot, and the boss's car was still there. Derek was torn between wanting to stick to his plan of leaving after his boss and meeting some friends to get on with the weekend activities. He decided to hang in there and was extremely happy when finally, around 6:30, the boss poked his head in the door and invited him to go have a beer. On the way to the local watering hole, Derek was congratulating himself that, after only one month on the job, he was already becoming buddies with the boss! (Proof that his strategy was working.)

While waiting for their drinks to be served, the boss was uncharacteristically quiet. When the beer arrived, the boss asked Derek a series of questions: "Do you like to drink beer, Derek?" Somewhat puzzled, Derek replied, "Sure." "Do you like this place?" Derek said, "Yes, it's fine." "When you let your hair down and want to relax a little bit, where do you go?" Derek mentioned several of his favorite places. Then the boss said, "That's good to know, Derek, because that is what quality professionals do on Friday. They leave work on time and they go do whatever it is they like to do. I am not impressed with people who can't get their work done in a normal business day. Of course, there are times when staying late is necessary, and I really appreciate the people who are willing to do that, but not every day. It is the exception, not the rule. If it takes you longer to do the work that your peers can do in less time, I have hired the wrong person. Capable people do not have to stay late on Friday. So what is it, Derek? Are you going to work late or drink beer?" To which Derek replied, "I get the picture. I'll drink the beer."

Derek's boss was pretty perceptive. He knew how to tell the difference between the people who were getting it done and those who only *looked* like they were getting it done. Derek did not work for a micromanager.

When people are effective at what they do, it is unnecessary to then require them to prove that they are busy. Monitoring the right things—successful outcome, cost-effectiveness, quality standards, deadlines—makes perpetual motion meaningless.

Restrictions on Process

People who use monitoring and reporting inappropriately are often evaluating compliance of the restrictions they have placed on people or the process. They tell you what you cannot do and then monitor to be sure that you are not doing it! They do not look for indications of compliance; they monitor for indications of violation.

> *I want you to solve this problem, but you can't talk to the people in HR.*

> *You need to discuss this with the client, but don't travel.*

> *I need you to reduce next year's budget by 10%, but you can't reduce expenditures in these three areas . . . .*

Micromanagers are driven to monitor negatives.

Monitoring Short-Term Costs versus Outcome or Long-Term Impact

The monitoring by micromanagers also focuses on short-term gains. Some examples:

- Changing an employee's air travel plans to a cheaper flight that arrives at 3:00 in the morning, disregarding the negative impact of his having to make an important presentation at 8:00 the next morning without the proper rest

- Refusing to allow someone to attend a training class because she is too busy or it is too expensive, without considering the positive results of improved efficiencies

- Purchasing inferior-quality, cheaper materials without considering the impact on long-term quality, product, or service

"Pennywise and pound foolish" is a good adage that describes the micromanager.

Monitoring Limited Indicators, Not Outcomes

The monitoring of specific indicators that are convenient and easy to assess is a tool of micromanagers. Rather than drilling down to the depth necessary to ensure relevant information from meaningful data, they use superficial data and make incorrect evaluations.

The monitoring of "averages" can be an example. While averages are relatively easy to monitor, they are frequently misleading. They do not identify specific occurrences that may "skew" the average. Averages create false positives or false negatives.

The Micromanaging Mayor

The mayor of a city of approximately three hundred thousand people had a rocky relationship with the city's police chief and the police department.

For example, the mayor devised a plan to hold individual police officers more accountable for their behavior. He instituted a policy that all complaints filed against individual police officers would immediately be made public. The local media and citizens would have readily available to them statistics tracking the number of complaints filed against each individual officer. This was the mayor's attempt to make government more transparent and expose any patterns of negative behavior by the city's police officers. While the details of the actual complaints were confidential and would not become public record, the actual number and nature of the complaints would be publicly monitored.

The goal was to identify those police officers whose behavior generated complaints from the taxpayers. The problem, or the monitoring flaw in the mayor's plan, was that the results of the complaint investigations were not made public. Therefore, if an officer had one complaint filed that was determined to be valid, that individual actually looked better than an officer who had ten complaints filed, with all of them being dismissed as having no merit. The plan measured the wrong thing—illusion versus reality!

The police chief and the police officers union reacted very negatively to this tracking system, feeling it unduly punished officers who were merely doing their job. In a memorandum to the mayor, the police chief pointed out that the policy of making the number of complaints public would cause the police officers to resort to an "emergency response mode" rather than pursue the necessary activities of preventive policing. The chief stated, "Many times when an officer is doing his or her job, by the nature of what they do, citizens may file a complaint. No one is happy when they get a speeding ticket or a member of their family attracts police attention. In many instances, preventive, day-to-day law enforcement runs the risk of citizens being upset and filing complaints. If the validity of the complaints is not reported, more citizens may be encouraged to complain, knowing that these allegations will have a negative impact on the officer involved." (This was now a great way to inflict retribution on an officer who did something someone did not like.)

The chief predicted, "Officers will be prone to abandon active policing and respond to emergencies only, much like the fire department and emergency medical response teams. If there is an event, the officers will respond, but they will shy away from the preventive activity that stops events from happening. They won't run radar, but they obviously will respond to auto accidents."

The chief went on to recommend that the outcome of the complaint investigations was a much more meaningful figure to track. That way, officers would only be held accountable for the complaints that were discovered to have merit. She said, "I have no opposition to officers being held accountable for any negative events that happen. I have serious opposition to the tainting of individuals or the entire department by allegations that may be unfounded. This plan violates any standards of innocence until proven guilty."

The mayor, while well intended, was micromanaging the process by measuring and monitoring the wrong indicators. It certainly would not be in the best interest of the community's citizens to create any circumstances where police officers were reluctant to do their job.

THE FREQUENCY OF MONITORING AND REPORTING

Reporting, while a necessity of organizational life, can be taken to extremes. Here is an example of inappropriate peer-to-peer monitoring and reporting.

Susan worked for a large nonprofit organization for over two years. She was involved with the gala year-end fund-raising event. The evening includes dinner, dancing, an auction, and inspiring speeches for the group's largest donors. Thirty percent of the funds raised by the organization come from this single event. (Obviously, it is a very high priority for the organization.)

Susan described herself as the "event team gopher." "I always picked up the loose ends for everyone else and made sure that nothing fell through the cracks," she said. "Whatever needed doing I did."

One year Susan was assigned to head the entertainment and silent auction portion of the event. Julie, who was responsible for this portion of the event in past years, gave Susan a list of agencies they have used in the past to secure entertainment and an extensive list of merchants that have been generous with donations for the auction. Susan was very appreciative of Julie's efforts; however, that year the theme for the event was very different. They were looking for entertainment and donations that supported a Caribbean theme of "A Romantic Night in the Islands." They wanted to secure as many auction donations as possible with an island theme (art, clothing, trips, etc.). Many of the merchants who had previously donated did not provide products or services that apply. That year the organization would have to find a lot of new sources.

Julie was insisting that Susan contact all past agencies and merchants and to give her a daily report on all of her progress; however, as mentioned, the past contacts did not necessarily support this year's theme. Julie appeared to be frustrated with Susan's lack of progress. She didn't think that Susan was doing things right. Susan was extremely frustrated because, she said, "Julie kept hounding me to contact the people who can't give us what we want. She also expected these daily updates that drove me crazy. I became upset that she kept telling my boss that I wasn't following up and doing the things that I was supposed to do. I really felt like I was caught between a rock and a hard place."

Julie was attempting to micromanage the process to the point of interference. She was inappropriately demanding information with such frequency that Susan did not have time to actually do the job. Julie's "help" was a hindrance.

MONITORING THROUGH BACK CHANNELS

Micromanagers are adept at developing alternative forms of monitoring or gathering information. It is not uncommon for supervisors or lower-level managers to discover that the people they manage are informally reporting to micromanagers several rungs up on the organizational ladder that have left the position but continue to monitor "how things are going" in their past area of influence.

Many micromanagers will defend this by calling it an open-door policy. In reality, it is not the front door that is open; it is the back door or a secret entrance to the basement.

SURVEILLANCE ACTIVITY

People who micromanage are usually big supporters of methods for tracking employee misbehavior and policy abuses. They want to keep tabs on people. Without a doubt, in some circumstances of heightened security and extreme confidentiality, these methods are necessary and appropriate. However, micromanagers often overuse these mechanisms, which is reflective of their belief that people will only work if they know they are being watched. At times, micromanagers use the guise of security to justify unnecessary extremes in tracking other people's activities.

UNSUPPORTIVE OF TELECOMMUTING AND WORKING FROM REMOTE LOCATIONS

Anything that takes people out of their immediate work environment, where they cannot easily be monitored, is anathema to micromanagers. If people are not present where they can keep an eye on them, there is an assumption of nonproductivity.

Micromanagers have no interest in telecommuting. They feel compelled to be where the action is and to engage in visible activity. If they are working remotely, they perceive that they are being left out or are unaware of day-to-day, minute-to-minute developments. For them, it creates an uncomfortable disengagement or disconnect with others.

In reality, telecommuting, or working remotely, does incur a cost of disconnectedness. Many people are highly productive working in such an independent manner, yet there is a price to be paid through lack of interaction and loss of engagement. For many, this situation is perfectly acceptable; for micromanagers, it is not.

THE NEGATIVE IMPACT OF DYSFUNCTIONAL MONITORING AND REPORTING

This micromanaging behavior contributes to a gradual, yet steep, erosion of productivity, efficiency, morale, and the job satisfaction of others. The negative impact compounds over time. The longer it goes on, the more damaging it becomes.

Decreased Productivity and Quality

The monitoring activity and reporting requirements can become so pervasive that people do not have the time to do their work. Instead of creating the quality and volume of work of which they are capable, they contribute less because the time to do the job is lost due to monitoring and reporting requirements.

Fear-Based Behavior Escalates

Behaviors grounded in fear abound. Increased telling of untruths, "extra efforts" disappearing, domination of CYA (cover your anatomy), high AT&T (absenteeism, tardiness and turnover), and obsequious behavior are some examples.

Micromanagement Assessment

■ *Is dysfunctional monitoring and reporting an issue?*

	YES	No
1. Are people required to give you reports or information that you don't have time to review?		
2. Do you monitor outcomes and results as opposed to activity?		

	YES	No
3. Have you ever practiced MBBSS (managing by becoming second skin)?		
4. Are you confident that what other people are doing won't somehow make you look bad?		
5. Are you an "I'll know it when I see it" kind of person?		
6. Do you believe that what people are doing right is as important as what they are doing wrong?		
7. Evaluate this statement: The champions of the workplace are the ones who are the first to arrive and the last to go home.		
8. When others take the time to think, plan, and prioritize, are they really being effective?		
9. Is following the standard process more important than increased quality and efficiency?		
10. Have you ever been told that you monitor "minor" or counterproductive factors rather than the major/important indicators?		

	Yes	No
11. Are frequent check-ins necessary to keep abreast of what is going on?		
12. Do you find it necessary to develop information through back channels or alternative sources?		

"Yes" responses to questions 1, 3, 5, 7, 9, 10, 11, and 12 or "no" responses to questions 2, 4, 6, and 8 indicate opportunities for self-evaluation.

You Might Be Micromanaging If . . .

You insist on multiple e-mail and voice mail updates throughout the day and then erase them because you are too busy to respond.

Every time people look up from their workstation, they see your eyes.

Your favorite word is *but*.

You have ever criticized someone for coming back five minutes late from the first lunch break he or she has taken in two weeks.

You have ever called a meeting to discuss the increased usage of Post-it notes and black felt tip pens.

You assign something to someone and follow up twenty minutes later to see how things are going.

Preliminary Micromanagement Behavior Inventory

As we move to Part III, it may be beneficial to retake this instrument. Based on the information in chapters 1 through 6, would you change any of your initial responses?

■ *Which of the following behaviors have you experienced in these three areas? (Check all that apply.)*

BEHAVIORS	MANAGERS/ SUPERVISORS	PEERS/ TEAMMATES/ OTHERS	SELF
Dominance, control, or disruption of your time?			
Attempts to impose their will by use of raw power or authority?			
Consistently having to "win"?			
Complete control over how things must be done?			
Requiring excessive, unnecessary approvals of tasks or decisions?			
Intense monitoring of your activities?			

BEHAVIORS	MANAGERS/ SUPERVISORS	PEERS/ TEAMMATES/ OTHERS	SELF
Excessive, unnecessary, redundant reporting requirements?			
Refusal to delegate?			
Refusal to accept collaboration?			
Incomplete, unclear, or distorted information?			

PART II
Dealing with
the People Who
Micromanage You

*What to do when you
are the MicromanagEE*

■ Symptoms of Being Micromanaged by Managers

1. You have little to no influence over how your time and efforts are invested.
2. You are consistently interrupted to respond to urgent requests by management.
3. There is always a "crisis of the moment" that shifts priorities and interrupts your scheduled work.
4. In assigning tasks, managers use terms similar to "Do it because I told you to and I am the boss."
5. Arbitrary changes are often made based on convenience or benefit to the manager.
6. Directions are given that run counter to existing policies, procedures, and guidelines without explanation or clarification.
7. Managers exercise complete control over how things are done.
8. When change is introduced, how the change is to be accomplished is mandated from above.
9. Problems tend to be solved based on how managers have responded to similar situations in the past.
10. You do not have authority commensurate with your responsibilities and accountability.
11. Even low-level decisions or action steps must be approved by managers before you can proceed.
12. Management expectations of goals and outcomes are unclear.
13. You spend a great deal of time creating reports that you are sure nobody ever reads.
14. Redundant information is required in multiple reports or different formats.

15. Excessive reporting requirements interfere with your ability to do your job.

16. Explanations and expectations for delegated tasks and projects are not clearly communicated.

17. Nonessential busywork tasks are regularly delegated or passed along to others.

18. Management regularly fails to listen to your ideas and suggestions.

19. Unnecessary attendance of meetings is mandated.

20. The criteria for making decisions is inconsistent and unclear.

Positive identification with six or more of these symptoms confirms micromanagement.

■ Symptoms of Being Micromanaged by Peers, Team Members, or Coworkers

1. Do others repeatedly interrupt your activities for help on their priorities?

2. Do others demand significant amounts of your time inappropriately?

3. Are you pulled away from your responsibilities on a regular basis to support people in unrelated parts of the organization?

4. Do others retaliate if you do not support their ideas and suggestions?

5. Do others constantly attempt to prevail or "win" in situations rather than compromise?

6. Are your ideas and suggestions regularly ridiculed or dismissed?

7. Do others demand that collaborative tasks be done "their way"?

8. Do past methods tend to prevail over innovation and creativity?

9. Is collaboration hindered if you suggest new ways of accomplishing something?

10. Do others want you to seek their agreement before you begin certain steps in your tasks and responsibilities?

11. Have others made changes in your work process without notifying you?

12. Do others make decisions that impact your performance without your input?

13. In collaborative efforts, are listening and the gathering of group input dominated by specific individuals?

14. Do others make inappropriate comments about your scheduling or compliance with policies and procedures?

15. Do others report your mistakes or challenges to management before you do?

16. Do others seem to change the rules frequently in collaborative efforts?

17. Are others hyperprotective of their "turf"?

18. Do others attempt to exert inappropriate influence in your areas of responsibilities?

19. Are you held more accountable than others for problems and challenges that occur in collaborative efforts?

20. Do others regularly take individual credit for cooperative achievements?

"Yes" responses to seven or more of these questions indicate a probability of micromanagement.

7

■ ■ ■

The Response to
Being Micromanaged

Throughout chapters 7 and 8, we will be discussing realities and strategies for micromanagEEs—those who are being micromanaged. These people will be referred to as "EEs."

KEEPING IT REAL

There are four realities in dealing with the people who micromanage. All four are predicated by the important fact that you have to take personal responsibility for dealing with the situation. No one else is going to correct the micromanagement problem for you. Whining and complaining, while perhaps understandable, will yield zero tangible results. Unfortunately, in today's workplace many people would rather complain about their situation than do something about it. Do not join that crowd. If you are already there, get over it and move forward.

The four realities are as follows:

- You do not have to be a victim of micromanagement

- It is not about fixing "them."

- Focus on what the situation is, not what it "should" be.

- Exercise influence over that which you have influence over.

You Do Not Have to Be a Victim of Micromanagement

Victims are people who have no options. When you are being micromanaged by managers, peers, team members, or coworkers, you have options. In both this chapter and the next, successful strategies will be offered to help you exercise some measure of control. You do not need anyone else's permission to begin the corrections. In many cases, there are unilateral actions that do not even require cooperation from others. You can implement them on your own.

Obviously, the most extreme option is to leave your current position. That may ultimately prove to be your best move. However, before you take such a drastic step, make every attempt to improve the situation. If you pack up and go, they win! Moving on without attempting to fix the situation is running from the problem. Chances are, if you do not learn to react effectively now, you will experience similar micromanagement behaviors in the future. There will be micromanagers no matter where you go.

It Is Not about Fixing Them

Chances are pretty high that you will not be able to "fix" the people who are micromanaging you. You probably do not have the authority or influence to compel them to change their behaviors. If you did, you would have already done it! What you do have total authority and influence over are your own actions and reactions. It is not the experiences of your life that define you; it's your reactions to those experiences that literally shape who you are. It is not what happens to you; it is how you choose to deal with it.

You may have to take some responsibility for the micromanaged situation. In both our personal and professional lives, we frequently teach people how to treat, manage, and interact with us. Perhaps unknowingly, your past reactions to people's micromanagement activities have encouraged their behavior.

Aaron was a high-performance employee who presented significant management challenges. When I assigned tasks to Aaron, he consistently responded with predictable, patterned behavior. He would complain that I was treating him unfairly. He would tell me he was overburdened and moaned that I always assigned all of the difficult work to him. Aaron perceived that he was being abused by being singled out to do the heavy lifting for the whole group. My predictable response was to increase the pressure, and as a result, Aaron would perform and do what I asked. I would tell him, "It was up to him to do whatever was necessary to make sure the job got done. I wanted results, not complaints. He was not being treated unfairly so get over it. The reason I give him the challenging tasks is because he is capable of achieving them."

Our pattern became, "I assign . . . He complains . . . I pressure . . . He performs." It was a dance that we would do.

Then one day Aaron came into my office in a very agitated state. He was visibly stressed and blurted out, "Things have to change around here because it just isn't working!" I replied, "Tell me what's not working." He said, "You keep burying me with work and I just can't handle it anymore." My response was "I think it's working fine. It may not be working for you, but it's working fine for me. I assign work, you complain, I step up the pressure, you perform. Tell me what isn't working."

Understandably, Aaron was unhappy with how he was being managed. While I am willing to take my share of the responsibility, in truth, he was a willing partner in creating the very situation that he found unworkable. From my point of view, Aaron had taught me how to manage him.

The outcome was that we negotiated a specific strategy for Aaron to communicate clearly when he was truly over-loaded. We also identified methods for prioritizing his responsibilities and how Aaron could secure help from others when it was necessary. Until Aaron changed his reactions to my management of him, I continued to treat him in the same old way. When it became apparent that this strategy was no longer effective, I altered my behavior.

You have a choice. You can be the equivalent of Aaron, the whiner and complainer, or Aaron, the individual who took the empowered action of altering his own reaction to create a more acceptable outcome—and do it before meltdown!

Focus on What the Situation Is, Not What It "Should" Be

Do not bog yourself down in lamentations of how things "should" be. Focus on the current reality. Separate the "is" from the "should." Unfortunately, all of us can get wrapped around the axle of righteous indignation and emotionally invest in our preconceived notions of how things should or should not be. *Should* reflects our personal opinion of perfection and is usually sculpted to benefit self. *Is* reflects the baseline of reality. Get rid of statements like these:

She shouldn't *treat me that way.*

It should *be different in our department/team/area.*

He should *have a different management style.*

I shouldn't *have to do that.*

This isn't how that project should *be done.*

Focusing on *should* saps your energy and creativity. Assess your current situation as it truly is, then determine the reactions and strategies that you believe will yield the most favorable outcomes. Dealing in the real world is much more beneficial than existing in the make-believe world of *should*.

Exercise Influence over That Which You Have Influence Over

You cannot change everything; some factors are way beyond your control. Prioritize your actions and focus your efforts in areas where you can produce results. This exercise will help put your situation into perspective.

The following is a five-step exercise known as the CUP Analysis. It is used extensively by individuals and organizations to separate controllables from uncontrollables and to prioritize strategies.

Step 1: Create a list of all of the positive and negative factors that impact your ability to do your job.
Your list will include, but not be limited to, the *specific* micromanagement behaviors of managers, peers, and teammates. Other factors such as the availability of resources, budget constraints, availability of training, and personal, non-work-related issues should also be included. Identify as many factors as you can; be creative and thorough. It should contain a minimum of twenty-five items with no maximum limitations.

Step 2: Categorize each individual factor, using the CUP criteria.

C—Identifies factors over which you have total control.

U—Identifies factors that are totally uncontrollable. You have no influence at all.

P—Identifies factors over which you have partial control or at least some measure of influence. Partial control is a large category with varying degrees of influence. This category may indicate significant yet not total control, or it may reflect a minimal amount of influence. Either way, partial control indicates that there are things you can do to exert some measure of influence over that factor.

While the specific micromanagement behaviors of managers and others is certainly a U (something that is uncontrollable), your *reaction* to their behaviors is a C, or at least a P. (Reality probably dictates a P rating. Most of us do not have total control over all aspects of our reactions.) So every uncontrollable micromanagement behavior will probably be responded to by a partially controlled reaction.

Typically, what you will find when completing the analysis is this: Very few things are rated C. It is a fact of life that we do not have total control over most of the factors in our professional or our personal lives. A C rating reflects complete authority, responsibility, and accountability. C ratings address competence. If you control something and it is successful, then obviously you are very competent. If you control it and it is unsuccessful, you have no recourse but to look in the mirror.

There will probably be a marginal amount of U ratings (truly uncontrollable factors). A high number of legitimate U ratings indicates victimization. The perception of uncontrollables may be rooted in fiction or fact. Feeling sorry for ourselves, we pout and lament the fact that there is nothing "poor me" can do. In some cases, it is just easier to see ourselves as victims; it absolves us of any responsibility for correction. Victimization can be comfortable. If, in fact, a high number of uncontrollables do truly exist and have a negative impact on your performance, you may wish to consider changing jobs. That is always one option or one area of influence over which you do have control. If you have rated a significant number of factors a U, please go back and reassess. If they are still rated a U, then it may be time to make some tough decisions.

In most cases there will be a very high number of P factors. These identify your true opportunities for success. One of the greatest factors of success in today's workplace is how well individuals, groups, and total organizations deal with the partial control factors in their environment. What makes one individual more successful and capable than another is frequently determined by the fact that he or she is better at dealing with the partial control factors in their environment.

When you rate something a P, you have one of two choices. You can (1) throw your hands up in frustration and say, "Poor me, I don't have control over this," or (2) commit to exerting the maximum possible impact and influence over everything that you can to the greatest extent possible.

Step 3: Acknowledge the uncontrollables and move on.

If they are truly uncontrollable, there is nothing you can do about them. Any time or effort consumed in thinking, talking, or fretting about factors over which you have no control is wasted time and effort. It is a waste of your most valuable resource: you! Kiss the uncontrollables good-bye. Acknowledge them and send them on their way. There is nothing you can do about them.

Step 4: Prioritize your partial control factors by rating them in importance and immediacy of opportunity.

Use the following rating structure:

1—Indicates an immediate or urgent opportunity. This is something that could or must be addressed as quickly as possible.

2—Intermediate-term opportunity (six months to one year). While immediate response would be welcomed, it is not urgent at the moment.

3—Long-term opportunity (one year or more). This is a factor that can be addressed over a longer period of time. The importance or urgency is not immediate.

It is very possible that a P-rated factor could have diverse elements that may be rated 1, 2, or 3, all within the same factor.

Step 5: Develop and commit to strategies that will address your 1, 2, and 3 partial control factors.
The remainder of this chapter and chapter 8 offer some strategies that will be helpful. Choose those you determine will work best for you; not every strategy works for every individual or in every situation. Dedication to continued implementation of the strategies you select is paramount. Trying something one time and then dismissing it because it was not totally effective will not yield meaningful results. You have to be willing to practice and take risks if you truly want to change your micromanaged situation. As in most first-time efforts, chances are great that you will not be immediately successful. Unfortunately, some people will assume that these strategies work for others but not for them. Other people will assume they are not capable of implementing

them effectively or that the people micromanaging them are much different than the people who micromanage everyone else. All of these interpretations predetermine failure. Choosing not to apply a strategy because you are convinced it will not work for you is a safe, low-risk behavior that will only perpetuate your current situation. Change equals risk. If you are sincerely committed to making a difference, continue reading.

The inventory of strategies, options, and responses begins with discovery.

DISCOVERY

Consider going right to the heart of the problem and discovering the micromanager's motive or rationale for the behaviors. The key skill here is structuring inquiries that will result in meaningful responses. There is no guarantee that micromanagers will engage the dialogue or be forthcoming with their answers; however, it never hurts to try. If you can find out what it is they are trying to accomplish or avoid, you may be able to offer alternative methods for success.

I would not recommend confronting the micromanager with a question such as "Why do you feel compelled to micromanage me/us/the situation?" That will probably elicit a volcanic response of denial and defensiveness! Effective inquiries are structured around three factors: interests, outcomes, and options.

Interests

Attempt to surface micromanagers' true interests in the project, task, or activity. What is most important to them?

- To address the political interests of themselves or others?
- To make themselves or the department/team/group look good in the eyes of someone else?
- To demonstrate their ability to lead something effectively?

Interests run deeper than just accomplishing goals. If you can discover their primary interests, you can lessen their perceived need to micromanage by increasing your responsiveness to those interests. You can be a contributing partner if you know what it is they would like to achieve. Interests go way beyond "just getting the job done." Everyone has an agenda; you do, and so does the micromanager. Agendas are not necessarily negative. Discover their interests and do whatever you are willing and able to do to help accomplish them.

Inquiries such as these may be helpful:

Along with getting the job done well, what additional interests need to be met?

Are there any risks or threats involved of which I need to be aware?

How will your interests and the interests of the group/team/department best be met in this project/task/activity?

Are there any political or under-the-radar factors in-volved other than meeting time, budget, and dollar requirements?

Outcomes

What outcomes are important to the micromanager? Out-comes tend to be hard, measurable results. Outcomes also contain negative factors. Attempt to discover the outcomes micromanagers do not want, which may prove more im-portant than the outcomes they profess to want. Possibly it is the presentation of the final report that is most impor-tant to them, not just the completion of the task.

Inquiries such as these can be helpful:

Are we competing with something else of which I should be aware?

What is the most beneficial outcome from this project?

What negative outcome could potentially be damaging?

What is the outcome that we want to avoid?

What should the final outcome look like?

Options

Once interests and outcomes are identified, offer input into the possible ways they can be achieved. This is the identifi-cation of methodology. If the micromanager is the only one who knows the interests and outcomes, he or she will be adamant in attempting to influence the methods used to accomplish the desired conclusion. However, when in-terests and outcomes are shared and you have a complete understanding of the objectives that are in play, you now become a partner in considering *how* things can be done. Micromanagers will put greater trust in your ideas of "how" if they perceive that your input is inclusive of their interests and outcomes.

Inquiries such as these are helpful:

What are the options that will accomplish the interests and outcomes that we have discussed?

How can I be of most help in making sure the interests and outcomes are met?

I would recommend these options. What do you think?

How many different ways are there to skin this cat?

Offer reasons why new or different methodologies would be in the *best interest of micromanagers*. If another way of doing things would benefit their interests and outcomes or decrease the likelihood of a negative result, they may be willing to consider your input.

This discovery process allows you to position yourself as an ally of the micromanager, not an adversary. You become an asset. If you demonstrate a willingness to support their interests and outcomes, micromanagers do not continue to see themselves as solo acts.

Whenever possible, do not limit your suggestions and recommendations to only one option. Offer multiple options (the optimal number is three), and engage micromanagers in discussions of which is actually the best choice. The selection process allows them to own the input. They can take credit for deciding which methodology to use.

While it is your input, they will probably want to take credit for it!

Be cognizant of the micromanager's sensitivity to your input on options with possible risks. Start off slow. It is not wise to inject yourself immediately into the methodology of a high-risk process. Any problems or mistakes could be very costly. Micromanagers will be intensely resistant to such risk and very protective of perceived intrusions into their space. They are likely to display a much greater willingness to entertain your input on options in less sensitive, less risky projects, processes, and tasks. Suggesting things with a positive impact in lesser-risk situations can get you some traction. When you have generated some success, you can begin to offer, and they may be more willing to accept, your help with the major challenges.

STRATEGIES, OPTIONS, AND FACTORS OF AWARENESS

The effective responses to micromanagement are all influenced by the following factors.

Be Aware of Their Need to Win

It is very important to pick your battles. You must decide when it is worth bucking the micromanager and when it is best to go with the flow. Micromanagers tend to press or pursue every issue. Do not try to match them, or you may become them! Initially address only the issues that are truly important to you or the process. Once you have a few early successes and the micromanager reaches an awareness that you are not attacking him or her personally, the relationship should begin to improve dramatically.

When you believe that an issue must be addressed, do not stake out a position in direct opposition to the micromanager. Use their stated position as a platform to build upon whenever possible. In most cases, a resolution must contain some elements of their recommendations.

Your goal is not to placate or improve your relationship by acquiescing. However, there are times when the micromanager will have to win.

Contending or taking an adversarial position is usually unproductive. It escalates micromanagers' negative emotions and contributes to discussions becoming personal very quickly. This is really the difference between *but* and *and*. Following their statement with a *but* tends to pick a fight. Using the word *and* to build upon, develop, or expand their ideas is much more productive. It is the paradox of tearing down or building up. Do not tell them they are wrong; tell them they are right, and then add on to it. Your input or influence on the process will increase when you position it as an addition to the micromanager's input. Make your input an "add on," not an "instead of."

Use "Hypothetical" References

Raise the level of discussion and reduce the personalization through the use of hypotheticals. Use phrases such as these:

Hypothetically, could there be another way of dealing with this problem?

In theory, could there be other ways of looking at this?

*Just suppose this strategy is not successful, then what
could we do?*

*To help me in my own growth and development, if there
were alternative strategies or additional options in dealing with this, what would they be?*

These statements invite micromanagers to expand their
view and thought process without being threatened. They
do not have to defend being right, and you are not seen as
questioning, challenging, or being oppositional. You are
not questioning their competence; you are seeking "growth
and development." Discussing hypotheticals or "what ifs"
gives them an opportunity to brainstorm without the need
to defend their position. Micromanagers usually respond
well to hypotheticals.

Always Assess the Risk of Going Over the Micromanager's Head

Frequently in dealing with micromanagers there is a temptation to "go over their head" to make others aware of your
problem and, hopefully, fix it for you. Be careful. When
you go over the heads of micromanagers, you take a serious risk. No one ever wants people to go above them, especially the micromanager who is driven by fear, comfort,
and confusion. Expect an intense, negative reaction and
probable retaliation if you do. This is a strategy of last resort; by going over their head, you are probably preparing
your own exit from the stage.

In chapter 8, we will consider some specific strategies
to counter the micromanagement behaviors of others.

8

■ ■ ■

Effective Strategies
for EEs
*Dealing with the People
Who Micromanage You*

The following additional strategies will be helpful in dealing with those people who micromanage. Whether they are people in formal management positions, peers, or team members, the strategies are applicable. While you may find some to be more comfortable than others, once again, I caution against assuming or predetermining failure. You do not know that something will not be effective until you try it.

APPEARANCES OF INERTIA AND INACTIVITY

Micromanagers quickly step in to fill any perceived vacuums. If they sense inactivity, any lack of forward motion, or stalled progress of any kind, they will take immediate steps to increase their influence, exercise some measure of control, and stimulate activity. Frequently their perception of the vacuum is either a lack of awareness of your activity or incomplete information on your progress. When micromanagers are comfortable and confident that

there are no misunderstandings concerning who is doing what,

progress is being made,

priorities are being addressed, and

timelines are being met,

their micromanagement behaviors subside. Help them obtain that comfort and confidence. How?

The Three-Step Process

Dealing with micromanagers can be broken down into three steps:

1. Preemptive anticipation
2. Preemptive anticipation
3. (You can probably figure this step out for yourself.)

Preemptive anticipation is probably the single most effective strategy you can initiate with micromanagers. Determine what information the micromanager needs to be comfortable and confident, then provide it *ahead of time*. Get out in front of information. Do not wait to be asked. *Take action to avoid their disruptive reaction.*

Some of the most effective uses of preemptive anticipation are described here.

A Monday Morning Update

This is a one-page, written summary outlining the current situation with all of your important responsibilities. This report communicates the following:

> *Awareness* You are establishing and reconfirming your awareness of high priority/important issues and recommitting to their achievement. *This makes the micromanager aware of your keen awareness!*
>
> *Reassurance* You are providing confirmation to micromanagers that you are focusing on the things that are obviously important to them. They do not have to micromanage; nothing will fall through the cracks. This increases their comfort and reduces their fear.
>
> *Timelines* You are acknowledging the interconnectedness of events and the deadlines that must be met. You are reinforcing your commitment to keep your agreements and deliver on time.

The Color-Coded "Stoplight Summary"

This is a list of all of your top priorities, color-coded by status:

> *Green* Means everything is a go, moving forward, no impediments.
>
> *Yellow* Indicates some caution. "There may be a problem and I may need some help. There could be some rough water here."
>
> *Red* Stop. "Something is broken, and it isn't being advanced or moved forward. We need to discuss this one as soon as possible."

Take the initiative to establish a meeting on any yellow or red items, and be prepared to provide additional information to demonstrate your understanding of the situation. (Obviously, the less yellow and red on your color-coded summary, the better!)

Beginnings and Endings

Provide timely updates in person, through e-mails, or by voice mail that indicate when you actually start and complete activities. Letting micromanagers know that you have begun something lessens their anxiety. Notifying them when something is completed gives them the comfort of knowing that closure has been achieved.

Demonstrate and Document Activity in the Micromanager's Absence

Micromanagers seem to have an inherent distrust that people will not be productive unless they are being closely monitored. Prove them wrong. When they are not present, for whatever reason, maintain or even increase your productivity. Submit a summarization of what you have accomplished upon their return (i.e., a one-page executive summary—"Update of Activities in Your Absence").

There will be a *very understandable* temptation to relax and not be as productive when micromanagers are absent. Their behavior makes you want to celebrate when they are gone! Fight that temptation. Doing so only reinforces their beliefs. You only prove them to be right and the micromanagement vise tightens.

Clearly Communicate Your Success and Follow-up

Document your successes. Take every opportunity to reinforce the micromanagers' awareness of the things you are doing well. If they ask you to follow up on something, close the feedback loop by communicating the outcome of your follow-up activity. Connect the dots for them; do not always assume that micromanagers will do the math. Your silence can be interpreted as a lack of success, unresponsiveness, or inactivity.

Lisa perceived that she was being micromanaged. She was consistently being questioned about things she had already completed. She was accused of not following up or carrying out her boss's directions, and it just wasn't true. Both she and her boss were very frustrated. Lisa decided to take a unilateral action to help alleviate this problem.

"Every Friday at the end of the day I compiled a report summarizing my week's activity. I realized that a lot of things were being accomplished, but the director just didn't know it. I titled the report 'Success and Follow-up.' In as few words as possible, I would number and identify the key things I had successfully completed that week. I identified the results of my follow-up activity on specific things she asked me to do. I created a three-column summary: 'Your Request,' 'My Response,' and 'The Result.'"

Lisa stated, "After a few weeks of submitting this 'Success and Follow-Up' summary, I found her starting to really back off. It was amazing. I felt like I could breathe again. It also helps me close out my work week and be able to mentally disconnect for the weekend. This is without a doubt one of the best things I have ever done to improve my job."

AVOID MAKING YOURSELF A TARGET

Do not make it easy for the micromanager to catch you doing something wrong.

Eliminate Misuse of Technology

In today's workplace, the most consistent policy violations involve the misuse of organizational technology: surfing the Internet, inappropriate telephone conversations, and so forth (some people actually run a home-based business during working hours using company technology).

Micromanagers always have their antennae up, trying to detect these kinds of violations. Do not make yourself a target. These activities are too easy to monitor; just don't do them. Prove to the micromanager that there is no need to monitor you closely in these areas.

Sensitivity to Time-Related Policies

Micromanagers are intensely focused on time. Before they say hello to you, they look at their watch to make sure you are on time. They know when you are late for work, from a break, or from lunch. It is a fact of life and you just have to learn to deal with it. Violating time-related policies in micromanaged environments, frankly, borders on being stupid. The policies are in place, they exist for a reason, and they have to be considered a condition of employment. When you accepted the job, you stated or implied your agreement to follow the rules.

If you stimulate the suspicion of micromanagers by violating technology or time-related policies, they assume that intense scrutiny of you in other areas is warranted and justified.

BALANCING THE DISRUPTIONS
IN YOUR TIME

Here are three strategies for neutralizing disruptions of time:

- *Offer input into deadlines.* Initiate discussions concerning timelines and deliverables. Be preemptive. If you hesitate, micromanagers will seize the opportunity to impose a deadline. Be the first to talk; offer your timeline before they impose a deadline.

  Tell them when you can do the task, not when you can't—for example, *"I can* have that by Tuesday," not "I *can't* do that now"; "I will start that *as soon as* I finish this"; "I *can't* possibly start that before I finish my current task."

- *Implement the USA technique for dealing with interruptions (Understand, Situation, Action).*

  "I *understand* this is important, and I'm anxious to work on it."

S—"Here is my *situation*. I have these three priorities that have to be done before the close of business today."

A—"What *action* should I take? Which one of these should I delay until tomorrow so I can focus on your new request?" or "Here is the *action* I recommend: I can begin work on that midmorning tomorrow and have it to you by 3:00." (Be proactive in establishing deadlines.)

Does the USA technique always work? No. Nothing works all of the time. However, if it is only successful one time out of ten, you have at least regained some control.

■ *Manage your meeting behaviors.* Be prepared. Know what information you need and what information you need to provide.

Do not create or support digressions. Stay focused and encourage others to do the same.

Do not pout. If the meeting is a reality, make the best of it. Do not negatively act out. It may only encourage the micromanager to prolong the meeting!

Offer to follow up online. Do not contribute to the necessity of another meeting. Suggest, "I will gather that information and send it to everyone electronically by the end of the day."

Commit to following up with specific individuals rather than requiring additional formal meetings.

ESTABLISHING EXPECTATIONS

As we have discussed, the expectations of people who micromanage are frequently moving targets. The bottom-line result is confusion. The confusion they create invites them to micromanage. (Go figure!)

There are a number of things you can do to have some measure of influence over unclear expectations.

Clarify Priorities

Every time you exit a conversation with a micromanager, you must have a clear understanding of the actual priority and importance of everything that was discussed. Many people find it helpful to negotiate a coding system. The system could be numeric, color coded, or word identified. Everyone must have the same understanding of what the classifications mean.

Designating something as a 1, red, or hot priority indicates "stop breathing and do this right now before you draw another breath."

Ranking something in the next category, perhaps 2, green, or midpriority, indicates that there is a cushion of time before it must be completed.

Rating something a 3, blue, or extended priority, indicates perhaps thirty days or more before its deadline.

Since it is necessary for you to soon "draw another breath," the 1, red, or hot priority item must be addressed immediately. Rating something at a mid- or lower level does not mean that it is unimportant; however, it does mean that other things take precedence.

Another similar technique is to ask the micromanager to summarize or conclude your conversation with their ranking of the items they have assigned. For example:

> *Of the four items that we discussed, how would you rank them in order of importance and urgency?*

> *Of these three tasks, which one should be done first and which one could be completed last?*

> *Of these activities, which one can we live with not being done immediately?*

Clarify Shifts in Priorities and Deadlines

Priorities and deadlines are always shifting. Number one hot priorities can cool in the face of changing demands. Yesterday's lesser priority can become today's emergency. You must negotiate a method for recognizing these shifts when they occur.

A continual part of your dialogue with people who micromanage must be the question "Are there any shifts in priorities and deadlines that I need to know about?" Do not wait for them to offer the information. Initiate these inquiries consistently throughout your workday. In both formal and informal conversations, it is never inappropriate to ask this magic question: "Are there any shifts in priorities and deadlines that I need to know about?"

When priorities and deadlines do change, and they will, seek clarification on how this impacts your other cur-

rent responsibilities. Invite the micromanager to help you
plan and prioritize your response to the change.

> *I understand that this priority has changed significantly.
> What activity should I suspend in order to get this one done
> sooner?*

> *Since this has become less important, what priority should
> I assign to my other tasks?*

> *I will set aside the other things that I am working on to
> take care of this escalating priority. Please understand
> that those other things will be delayed.*

Negotiate the Criteria for Evaluation

As we have stated throughout this book, it is very difficult
to meet an expectation when it is unknown. Assist micromanagers in being more specific in formulating and communicating their true expectations. In many cases, they are
not intentionally withholding a clear explanation; it is just
not completely clear to them yet. The important thing is to
aid them in clarifying the criteria they will use to determine the quality of the outcome. Clearly understood criteria is the key to meeting any expectation.

Perhaps these inquiries will help your clarification.

> *What criteria will you use to judge the success of this project?*

> *Help me understand what you are looking for and how
> you will define a successful outcome.*

> *Tell me three things you will be looking for to judge this
> [task], two things that you are very concerned about, and*

the one thing that will be most important in determining success.

The last time we did something similar, _____ was considered the most important. Is that still the case?

While all of these are important, is it time, cost, or quality that is the most sensitive issue on this task?

Create Your Own Paper Trail

Unless specifically told not to do so, summarize conversations, agreements, and instructions with informal, non-threatening e-mails and memos. These can be headed with statements such as these:

This reflects my perception of what I'm going to do to complete the project.

A quick summarization of my understanding of our conversation is . . . .

This summarizes my understanding of what we are going to do.

To follow up, this is your recommended action.

To reduce the potential for misunderstandings, it is smart to create as much documentation as possible. Take away as much of the gray area concerning priorities, deadlines, and expectations as you can. Once these things are established through a paper trail of summarization, it becomes more difficult (not impossible) for them to be continuously redefined.

It is pretty obvious that information plays a critical role in dealing with micromanagers. Seek it; offer it; take the "information initiative."

AUTHORITY/APPROVALS/DECISIONS

In dealing with those who micromanage, the goal is to reduce the requirements for approvals and increase your authority in making decisions to achieve assigned responsibilities. Approvals will never be entirely eliminated, and authority and decision making will never be absolute (you probably don't want it to be). The range between the two is an area of partial control where you can use your influence to accomplish change. Here are some strategies to help.

Learn from Others

Do other people in your immediate environment or within the organization seem to have more authority than you in similar situations? If so, try to find out why. Get past the initial reaction of "The boss likes them better. . . . I am being treated unfairly."

What is it about them or their situation that is different? Is there something you can do differently? Can you learn from the "best practices" of others?

Need versus Want

Authority and decision-making capabilities are external struggles. Micromanagers want you to have less and you want more. It is important to focus on what you *need* to be more efficient and productive versus what you *want*. *Need* is process and performance driven; *want* is typically ego driven and related to the subordination of self discussion that we had in chapter 2.

Key questions include the following:

- What expanded level of authority that you currently do not possess would speed the process and make it more cost-efficient?

- What delays regularly occur in waiting for others to approve an activity or make decisions?

- What percentage of the approvals you are required to seek are actually declined or modified?

- Are there any required approvals that are really formalized check-ins or progress updates? While they may be necessary, could they be accomplished without slowing the process?

Your responses to these questions will provide valuable information for discussions and negotiations with micromanagers. The goal is to agree to alternative procedures that allow micromanagers to receive the information they crave without bottlenecking the process.

Consistent Process versus Variable or Unusual Tasks

Your greatest opportunity for aligning authority and decision making with your responsibilities is in the consistent tasks and repetitive projects in which you are engaged. The unusual or extraordinary things that you are required to participate in will lend themselves to more control by the micromanager. Analyze your repetitive tasks, and identify the required approvals that could be opportunities for eliminating slowdowns and expanding your authority and decision making.

Terri worked in the administrative office of a government agency. An important part of her job responsibilities was processing travel requests, requisitions for advances, and expense reimbursements. The traditional process was for her to compile a batch of requests for travel or payments and submit them in bulk to the chief administrative officer for approvals or denials. This was a cumbersome process resulting in frequent delays. Agency employees planning to travel or seeking reimbursement for expenses were regularly frustrated and unhappy. If travel requests were not approved on a timely basis, trips had to be canceled. This negatively impacted the customers the agency served.

Terri's boss, the chief administrative officer, had many different responsibilities and did not consider these requests and reimbursements to be a high priority. (Not his own travel requests and reimbursements, just the requests and reimbursements of others!) As a result, Terri was constantly fielding phone calls and e-mails from people who were waiting for action to be approved. Her typical response was "Let me see what I can do to move this along."

Terri decided to take the initiative. She began to track the percentages of the requests and reimbursements that were ultimately approved with no delay versus those that had encountered problems in the process. She discovered

*that less than 3% of requests either were denied or had reim-
bursements adjusted. She then analyzed any patterns that
contributed to delays, denials, or adjustments. What she
found was interesting. Problems resulted from two main
sources:*

> *Frequency of travel requests (If agency employees were
> requesting more than two travel approvals per quarter, or
> four in a given six-month period of time, these were
> delayed or denied.)*

> *Excessive expenses for airfare and lodging (people trying
> to fly first class or stay in five-star hotels, etc.)*

*Based on her findings, Terri offered the following proposal to
her boss. "Allow me to approve travel requests that do not
exceed two per quarter or four in a six-month period of time.
Anything in excess of that will be sent to you for your decision." She also asked for a threshold figure to be established
for lodging and airfare costs that would trigger further review.
For everything below that figure, she would have the authority to approve the reimbursement. She recommended compil-
ing a monthly report of all travel and reimbursement activity
for review by the chief administrative officer to insure the
compliance with this agreement. She proposed that the chief
administrative officer become involved in preapproving only
the exceptions. Situations falling within the norms of existing travel policies and patterns would no longer have to be
approved.*

Yes, there is a Santa Claus! The chief administrative officer agreed. Micromanagement of the approval and reimbursement process was dramatically reduced. As a result of Terri's initiative, welcomed changes were made.

In Part II, we have offered suggestions or actions you can take to lessen the impact of other people's micromanagement of you. Once again, you may not be able to change their behavior; however, you can change your reaction to their behavior.

✳ *You are not a victim.*

Focus on what the situation is, not what you think it should be.

It is not about fixing them.

Influence that which you have influence over.

In Part III, we address the options for not becoming an ER (a micromanagER).

■ Symptoms of Micromanagement

1. Others display a reluctance to be candid with you in their formal and informal reporting.
2. You feel confident that you have a good grasp on all of the minor details of the projects and tasks on which others are working.
3. You offer creative ideas on the nuts and bolts, day-to-day responsibilities of others.
4. Others attempt to keep their conversations with you short and superficial.
5. People seem resistant or reluctant to talk when you approach them in their work area.
6. People come to you with problems, not solutions.
7. Others seem unwilling to take minor risks without your approval.
8. You are frustrated because no one else generates new, creative ideas.
9. When you return from being away, people are anxious for you to clear your in box so that they can get on with their work.
10. Rather than thinking for themselves, people wait for you to tell them what to do.
11. In conversations with others, you do 90% talking and 10% listening.
12. People bring other work with them to do during your meetings.
13. Requests for training are low and you reject more requests than you approve.
14. Others seem unclear about priorities and goals and they are consistently requesting more information.

15. You focus more on what others are doing wrong than what they do right.
16. You assume others are comfortable when you win and they lose.
17. Your work ethic seems to be stronger than anyone else's.
18. When you ask for volunteers, no one raises their hand.
19. The people around you regularly miss deadlines.
20. Others constantly fail to meet your expectations.
21. Customers are complaining more about lack of responsiveness and slowness in addressing their issues.
22. Tardiness and absenteeism are high among the people you influence.
23. Others voice repeated complaints about boredom or being burned out.
24. You hesitate to go on vacation, attend meetings, or even take sick days because too much work will be piled up waiting for your return.
25. You experience retention problems at a higher than normal rate.
26. A significant number of people are leaving for "better opportunities."
27. Others do not offer updates or FYI data without you requesting it.
28. You have a backlog of reports from others that you haven't reviewed.
29. You are frustrated because of constant cell phone or pager interruptions.
30. You have a backlog of second-request e-mails needing information or action from you.

31. Others do not offer suggestions on "how" things should be done.
32. You are more frequently disappointed in the lack of intellect, creativity, and ability of those around you than you are ever impressed by their abilities.
33. You often feel frustrated that you don't have all of the information on the projects, tasks, and activities that people around you are responsible for doing.
34. Others are vague in their communications and carefully parse their words.
35. The people around you engage in a lot of blaming of each other.
36. You are concerned that information and decisions will somehow be leaked to others before you are ready for them to be informed.
37. The people you influence don't seem to understand decisions, procedures, and policies.
38. People seem to enjoy making others look bad.
39. Rumor, gossip, and the grapevine operate at substantially high levels.
40. People tend to go "unforgiven" for their mistakes over a long period of time (maybe forever).

PART III
Avoiding Becoming
the MicromanagER

*Symptoms of
Micromanagement*

9

■ ■ ■

Becoming a Micromanagement Buster
Neutralizing Your Own Micromanagement Behaviors

Throughout chapters 9 and 10, we will be discussing realities and strategies for micromanagers: those who want to reduce their own micromanagement behaviors. They will be referred to as "ERs."

Chapters 1 through 7 offered various assessments to determine whether you have a tendency for micromanaging and which of the micromanagement behaviors you may be demonstrating. In this chapter, we will begin to look at correcting those behaviors.

KEEPING IT REAL

To reduce, neutralize, or eliminate micromanagement behaviors, there are three realities in your area of responsibility:

awareness, willingness/commitment, and ability. Without them, no correction is possible.

Awareness

You must confront your micromanagement behaviors and acknowledge either the existence of or potential for those behaviors in your personal style. Lack of awareness is either a void of knowledge or denial. Having read chapters 1 through 7, you now have the knowledge. The micromanagement behaviors have been identified, defined, and exemplified. The denial part is up to you. If the micromanagement behaviors are still everyone else's problem but not yours, and you are convinced that you are not now, never have, or ever will be engaged in these behaviors, frankly, the next two chapters are not going to help you.

Willingness/Commitment

There must be a willingness and commitment to change existing or avoid future micromanagement behaviors. Without willingness, no change can occur. A teacher cannot teach an unwilling student. There has to be a willingness to start implementing new strategies, stop using counterproductive methods, and continue doing the things that enhance efficiency and productivity. Changing behaviors is a consensual activity. Your willingness and consent is mandatory.

Willingness occurs in ranges or degrees. Some things we are willing to change; others we are not. Many of your current strategies are obviously productive. Good. Commit to doing more of them. Some of your less productive behaviors are likely anchored in a belief that they are necessary or comfortable. Some of them you may be unwilling to let go of; others are easier to change. That's fine. Overcoming micromanagement is not about making an immediate 100% change in problematic behaviors. In many cases, it is about gaining ground by inches, and you must commit to gaining the ground!

Pick one or two specific behaviors to correct. Listen to others. What are you doing that impacts people negatively? Commit to meaningful change in those specific areas. Subsequent changes will be easier once you gain the momentum of success.

Ability

Ability can be developed. Awareness and willingness are internal issues; ability is both internal and external. Everyone has some level of baseline ability. Improved ability in any endeavor demands repetitive commitment. Whatever your current level of ability, start from there and move forward. Some engines need to be completely overhauled; others may need a minor tune-up. The information contained in this chapter and the next will help in all ranges of desired improvement.

Inherent in increasing ability is a willingness to take risks (there's that word *willingness* again!) and a commitment to practice. Learning something new or strengthening an existing level of skill never goes perfectly the first time. There must be a commitment to fail your way to success. There are those who will try something new one time and then abandon it when it does not go perfectly. If that is the case, you will not be successful in avoiding, reducing, or eliminating any of your micromanagement behaviors. You will quit the new behaviors quickly and revert back to your primary micromanagement style.

Do You Have What It Takes to Change?

Remember the formula from chapter 1?

$$Mm = Fr + Cm + Cf$$

We identified the drivers or causes of micromanagement as fear, comfort, and confusion. Any changes in these behaviors must address these three factors.

Fear

Micromanagement is a premature coping mechanism. The behaviors are intended to avoid that which you fear. Confront your fear. Do not manage by it. What is the outcome that you dread? Once you have identified it, ask yourself what the exact opposite is of what you fear. What is the outcome you want to achieve? Structure your behavior and influence people and situations toward achievement, not avoidance. Micromanagement is the equivalent of an athletic team that does not play to win; they play not to lose.

Micromanagement is a mechanism for avoiding problems as opposed to creating success. Focusing on the positive outcome as opposed to a feared result may sound like a minor, subtle nuance, but it is about as subtle as being run over by a freight train! Manage toward what you want, not away from what you fear.

Comfort

In leading others or working collaboratively, the issue is not about your comfort; it is about *collective* comfort and productivity. It is about others, not just you.

In the past, organizational models and managerial behaviors were very autocratic and authoritarian. People were expected to do what the boss told them to do. In the past it was important to make the boss happy. In the past people at the top inflicted methods that were comfortable and productive for them. Today we identify methods that are reasonably comfortable and productive for everyone who is involved in achieving an end result. Today it is important for people to enjoy their jobs. Today we focus on the collective benefit.

Chapter 2 dealt with the inability to subordinate self. The factor of comfort is right in the wheelhouse of that issue. If you are going to avoid, reduce, or eliminate the behaviors of micromanagement, you will experience some discomfort.

Confusion

Clearly identifying expectations, decision-making criteria, and explanations of requests, tasks, and responsibilities reduces confusion. Confusion is the condition that invites and rationalizes micromanagement. As confusion clears, micromanagement behaviors wither. Here are some suggestions for alleviating confusion:

- *Establish communication mechanisms that are consistent, timely, and accurate.* People need to understand how information will be delivered to them and have confidence that they are a part of the information loop. The methods for delivery must be dependable and not at the micromanager's whim.

- *Include everyone in direct communication.* To avoid the perceptions of unfairness or creation of an in-crowd versus an out-crowd, everyone must receive information at the same time or within the same reasonable time frame. When everybody gets the same information at the same time, it lessens the perception that others know more, know something different, or information is being intentionally withheld from an individual or group.

- *Do not devalue communication.* Do not routinely cancel group or individual meetings. It sends a message that individuals and communication are unimportant. If communication and information are treated as unimportant, confusion will become permanent.

- *Develop a realistic prioritization of information.* Not all information is red hot. If it is important, communicate that importance. If it is background only, let people know. Do not over- or underemphasize. Prioritize information realistically.

- *Communicate goals and objectives accurately.* Do not inflate to unrealistic or distorted levels. The people around you know what is realistic and what is not.

Establishing unrealistic goals usually results in a lessening, not an enhancement, of performance, and contributes to massive amounts of distrust.

Invest your energies and efforts in clearing up any confusion among the people you influence and the lure and the need to micromanage evaporates.

All of the strategies for avoiding, reducing, or eliminating micromanagement behaviors contain two universal components: negotiation and communication. Both have a common denominator, and that is listening. Listening is not a strong trait among micromanagers. To be a successful negotiator, you must listen to the other parties involved. Negotiation without listening is overpowering or rolling over others in the pursuit of surrender. Negotiation without listening is a one-dimensional process. It creates winners and losers, which ultimately degenerates into everyone losing. (Reluctant compliance or the pursuit of future payback positions the losers to be counterproductive to the desired outcome.) The goal of a true negotiation is to arrive at agreement, not to win or have others give in to you.

Communication without listening is merely a single-dimensional delivery of information. It is telling others what you want them to do, issuing orders, and expecting obedience. Communication without listening is demand-based talking.

Inherent in the communication process are explanation, teaching, and coaching. Understanding is the goal of communication. Agreement is not always necessary; understanding is essential.

Negotiation and communication combine to structure the single most effective strategy for eliminating micromanagement behaviors: establishing operating agreements.

CREATING OPERATING AGREEMENTS

Operating agreements are preidentified behaviors to address consistent and predictable circumstances. If you know something either is occurring now or may occur in the future, wisdom dictates that a thoughtful plan be predetermined for addressing the situation. Fire drills are a good example. There is the potential for fire to occur. Knowing this, do you wait until a fire breaks out before you try to figure out how to deal with it in the pressure of the moment? No! You anticipate that a fire may happen, identify the correct procedures for ensuring safety, then extinguish or contain the blaze and notify the fire department. If a fire never occurs, you have the peace of mind that your preparation may have helped prevent it. If a fire does occur, you are prepared with a predetermined response to the situation.

Operating agreements are your plans for dealing with your workplace fires and predictable circumstances. They are an opportunity to negotiate and communicate agreements that reduce or eliminate the need to micromanage.

Is it possible that, in your interactions with the people you directly influence or those you work with in collaboration, your interaction could be perceived as interference or disruption? Of course. Is it possible there will be excesses or misunderstandings in influencing and control of others' time? Determining methodologies? Requirements of approvals and decision making? Monitoring and reporting? Delegation and collaboration? Frankly, it is not only possible—it is guaranteed. These situations are predictable and consistent with all organizational experience. Get out in front of them. Address them before they happen by negotiating operating agreements as to how to deal with them when they occur—the response to the fire before the fire erupts.

Thomas Jefferson is credited with saying, "What you do when you don't have to determines what you will be when you can't help it." Establishing thoughtful operating agreement upfront reduces frustration, interference, and disruption when stress and pressure escalate.

Before we discuss operating agreements for the specific micromanagement behaviors, there is one exercise that can be implemented on a 360-degree basis. This exercise works with people who report directly to you, people you or your group or team support, as well as individuals or groups with whom you work collaboratively. If there is such a thing as a one-size-fits-all corrective strategy for avoiding, reducing, or eliminating micromanagement behaviors, this is it. This technique is called "Helps, Interferes/Disrupts, and Consider." I have used it both personally and shared it successfully with many consulting and training clients for years. It works!

Initially, dedicate about forty-five minutes for the exercise. Conduct an interactive discussion with each of the people you work with most closely. Ask a series of three questions. Notice that all of these statements end with a question mark. A question mark is an invitation to shut up and *listen!*

1. What do I do that *helps* you accomplish your goals, objectives, and responsibilities?

2. What do I do that *interferes with or disrupts* you in accomplishing your goals, objectives, and responsibilities?

3. What should I *consider* doing differently?

Effective operating agreements are forged from the response to question 3. In this exercise, you are inviting people to tell you what you are doing well (it is important to hear the good stuff). You are also inviting them to tell you whether they perceive you are micromanaging them in their performance. This gives others the opportunity to identify when the interference and disruption occurs from their viewpoint. Collectively, you can define when input becomes micromanagement.

In the third question, you are asking them for suggestions on how you can do things differently. There is no guarantee that you can or will implement their requests. The important thing is that you are actively seeking their input and *listening.*

With the benefit of this knowledge, you can begin to negotiate "going forward" operating agreements to address the problem areas. These agreements can follow the familiar Start, Stop, and Continue structure.

"Based on our discussion . . .

I will *start* doing this."

I will *stop* doing this."

I will *continue* doing this."

An important piece of the puzzle is identifying *how* any perceived violations of operating agreements will be raised. For example: "Let's agree on how to bring it to my attention if you perceive I am not keeping my agreements."

An additional positive outcome from this exercise is that you begin to uncover problems earlier rather than later. You find out about the mole hill before it becomes the mountain. Once you have asked the series of three questions, invite your colleagues to ask the questions of you. It gives you the opportunity to offer recognition of the good things they do and identify the things on their part that cause you to micromanage them.

Conduct this exercise on a regular basis, perhaps every ninety days or so (more frequently, if necessary). It contributes to building effective workplace relationships. Please keep in mind that the first few times you try this exercise, it will feel uncomfortable. Commit to doing it four times before you assume it does not work and abandon it.

SUBORDINATION OF SELF

In chapter 1, we discussed the challenge of subordination of self. Here are four suggestions that you may find helpful.

- *Determine the situational value of being right and winning.* You cannot fight every battle. Do not invest your personal capital and equity in the pursuit of issues that just are not worth it. If it is a significant issue, pursue it as intensely as possible. If not, learn to yield. Others have to win, too!

- *Eliminate "I told you so."* This is an ugly phrase, especially at the expense of making others look bad by showing them up. You are much more effective by feeding success, rather than rubbing people's noses in their failure and misjudgments. The gloating display of a micromanager proclaiming "I told you so" is a distasteful sight. Even if you are feeling it, keep it to yourself!

- *Honor the history of others.* Realize that others have history, too. Their experiences are as dear and valuable to them as yours are to you. The history of others can be a wealth of learning and can offer alternative ideas for you if you will allow it.

- *Exercise self-discipline and control.* Follow this advice especially concerning issues of disagreement, resistance, or the temptation to withhold support. Keep your own counsel. If you are in disagreement with organizational policies, decisions, or strategies, do not share it inappropriately. Complaints go up; they never go out or down. You do not have the right to spread your poison to others.

Be aware of temper tantrums. Actions such as shooting the messenger and nonverbal displays of displeasure or contempt may border on abuse. The apparent disregard of others by being abusive is one of the ultimate demonstrations of lack of self-subordination.

Lack of self-discipline and control damages careers—yours and others!

Kaia

Kaia is a design specialist for a clothing manufacturing company. The director of HR has asked her to serve on a cross-functional team to help make recommendations for changing the company's employee appraisal process. The company's executive group has committed to updating and equalizing the process by which employee performance is assessed, merit increases are determined, and promotional eligibility is established. The HR director wants input on proposed changes from people in all areas of the organization. A heavy emphasis is being placed on involving hourly and staff employees. Kaia has been with the company for over five years and believes that a change is necessary. She welcomes the opportunity to participate on the performance evaluation assessment team (PEAT).

Kaia reports directly to micromanager Sean, the director of fashion development. While he has given lip service to supporting Kaia's participation on the PEAT initiative, he is intensely opposed to any changes in the current performance appraisal process. He believes the process is fair and efficient. It has worked well for many years, and he personally has benefited from it (which just proves how well it really works).

Prior to her first meeting with the PEAT team, Kaia was summoned to Sean's office for a meeting. He instructed her to do everything she could to stop any changes in the current process. Even if new changes were recommended, he insists they be optional. Managers should have the choice to use the new guidelines or continue to conduct performance appraisals under the existing format. Sean's biggest concern is the measurement standards of any new evaluation program. He stated, "You can't always measure what we do here in the fashion development department. Some things in other areas can be easily measured, like how many garments are produced per day. In my area, it is impossible to measure specific outcomes. I need to have flexibility to subjectively rate my people's performance." (Sean has demonstrated a track record of subjectively rating higher the people he likes and subjectively rating lower the people he doesn't, regardless of actual performance.) Kaia and her peers are aware that the current rating system really boils down to Sean's opinion: "If he likes you, you are fine; if he doesn't, you are not."

Kaia dislikes Sean's subjective ratings system. She wants a more objective standards-based measurement system. She has some specific ideas on how to measure performance, but Sean has always dismissed them as unrealistic. Kaia also believes that if the ultimate recommendation of the PEAT is not reflective of Sean's position that she will be held negatively accountable. Sean expects Kaia to report to him the progress (or lack thereof) of the PEAT discussions.

Kaia has been asked to participate in the PEAT group to provide an independent voice for determining employee perspective and recommendations. The HR director does not want management dominance of this issue; however, Sean expects Kaia to carry his message and to create the outcome that he wants. He is involving Kaia in a conspiracy of sort to subvert the process of discussion and change. This lack of self-subordination extends to Sean using others, vulnerable to his influence, as his proxy. He expects her to subordinate both her own and the company's best interest in support of his own agenda.

Obviously, Sean is telling and not listening. He has not accepted input from Kaia and her peers in the past; he has always dismissed their comments as unrealistic. He now makes an assumption that Kaia either does or should see the world exactly as he sees it. You can imagine her frustration and resentment.

Sean can do several things differently.

- *Exercise his own independent voice.* He can request the opportunity to address the PEAT group himself. This would place his thoughts before the group and allow Kaia to function independently, as was the intention of the members of the group.

- *Create an operating agreement.* He can discuss his views with Kaia. Collectively, they can search for issues of commonality upon which they can agree. They can also discuss areas of disagreement and negotiate a way for his issues to have a voice. He can construct a letter summarizing his thoughts and ask Kaia to present it to the group. Perhaps they can agree that she would offer his perspective as the opposing view.

In chapter 10, we will address specific strategies to avoid being an ER.

10

■ ■ ■

Negotiating Operating Agreements

I n chapter 9, we discussed the importance of creating
operating agreements. In this chapter, we will look at
specific guidelines for doing this successfully. The strategy
of operating agreements is involving others in the methodology of *how* things will be done. It is giving others a stake
in their environment, an opportunity to be listened to, and
personal responsibility and accountability for their own
commitments.

Operating agreements can be created with individuals
and collectively with groups. They involve identifying
methods for interaction that enhance productivity and
efficiency.

CONTROL OF TIME

It may be necessary for you to have some measure of influence over how others are spending their time. This is typically a planning function. There are also situations when

other may have to be interrupted to address a pressing issue of the moment. How can this be accomplished with minimal interference and disruption? To avoid the micromanagement of others' time, consider the strategy described here.

The Communication

I need to have an understanding of how you are utilizing your time. It is helpful for me to know what priority you place on certain responsibilities, and I would like to feel comfortable that we are acting instead of reacting as much as possible. I do not want to plan your time for you, yet I need to know that effective planning is taking place.

The Negotiation

How can I be apprised without being intrusive of what you are planning and how you are investing your time?

How can I let you know when I think planning or time allocation could be improved?

How do you feel comfortable in letting me know when you need help in planning?

How can you let me know if you feel I am micromanaging your time?

The Agreement

Listen to their input, offer yours, and create an agreement that accomplishes your objectives and allows them to do their work with minimal interference. Structure the agreement by the Start, Stop, Continue format. Once the agreement is reached, give each other permission to make mistakes. Put a method in place where either of you can identify circumstances when it is believed that the agreement is being breached.

The Communication

There are times when I may have to interrupt what you are doing to ask for your assistance in dealing with a crisis or an important issue that may flare up. I also want to be responsive to the frustration that comes with these interruptions, and the disruption it causes in your other activities and responsibilities.

The Negotiation

What is the best way for me to notify you of the issue and ask for your assistance?

What can you do to make me aware of any support or assistance that you need?

How can I best communicate the substance and necessity of these types of interruptions?

If I perceive that these requests are not being followed up as quickly or completely as necessary, how can I let you know?

How can you communicate to me when these requests appear to be overburdening or unfairly assigned to you?

How can you communicate the impact this will have on your current activities and deadline requirements?

The Agreement

Listen to their input, offer yours, and create an agreement that accomplishes your objectives and with which they are comfortable. Consider teaching the USA technique for communication work overload from chapter 8. Negotiate an agreement. Commit to it, and identify how violations will be addressed.

The Communication

Meetings are necessary for us to share information, brainstorm problems, and make sure that everyone has the same knowledge and awareness of the challenges facing them.

Meetings can be an unnecessary evil. While it is important that we meet, we need to be aware that too many meetings or letting them run too long reduces our ability to do our jobs.

The Negotiation

What can we do to control the number and length of our meetings?

What can we do to be more efficient in our meetings?

What types of meetings do you find unnecessary?

How can we control meeting digressions?

How can you communicate to me when you think that meetings are unnecessary?

How can you communicate when you think a meeting is necessary?

How can we limit meeting attendance and not re-quire people to participate when the topic does not relate to them or their responsibilities?

The Agreement

Listen to their input, offer yours, and create an agreement that accomplishes your objectives and with which they are comfortable. Negotiate an agreement. Commit to it, and identify how violations will be addressed.

Additional Recommendations

Challenge your own comfort.

What is good for you or convenient at the moment may not be the same for others. You may be in a position that allows you to make authoritarian demands on others or provides opportunities to exercise raw power, but doing so, frankly, is a sign of weakness, not strength. Subordinate your own comfort and engage behaviors that increase the performance of others.

Evaluate your "impulse (brain cramp) of the moment." Is it really worth interfering or disrupting others in their current activity just to satisfy your immediate need? If so, what are you willing to accept less of from them? As you learned in chemistry class, for every action there is an equal and opposite reaction. You can't have it all!

Respect others' routines, methods, and perceptions of performance. Consider yourself 10% less and them 10% more, and make a significant impact on morale, job satisfaction, quality, and performance.

Increase clarity; reduce confusion.

Clearly establish priorities, goals, and objectives. Others can work independently with less input and interference when everyone has a clear understanding of what must be done.

Consider accumulating your requests and giving them to people at one time instead of interrupting someone five times with one request each time. Schedule a short discussion to present the projects all at once. Yes, it still adds to their workload, but it causes less interference and is more readily accepted.

Teach others the skills of organization and planning (pursue these skills yourself). You will be less compelled to exercise influence over other people's allocation of time if you have confidence that they are well organized.

DETERMINING HOW THINGS WILL BE ACCOMPLISHED

To what extent can you involve others in discussions and decisions concerning methods? This is a challenge for many managers. In today's workplace, people want to have influence over their environment, and they want to be heard. How can managers listen, empower others, and still meet the standards, goals, and objectives for which they are held responsible? As a manager, or when taking the lead on a project, task, or activity, it is of paramount importance to communicate the *W*s:

What we are going to do

Why we are doing it

When it must be completed, and perhaps

Who will be responsible for specific aspects (if more than one person is involved and there is a differentiation in activity)

Where the activity will take place

If you clearly communicate the *W*s and the criteria for expense allocation and the quality of outcome expected, you can frequently involve others in discussions of "how" all of this will be accomplished. In highly regulated environments, methodology may be mandated; however, there are always opportunities to seek input from others. As long as people stay within the white lines on the highway, the lane they drive in usually does not matter (as long as they drive safely and comply with existing laws).

The Communication (once the Ws are clearly established)

I don't have all the answers on the best way to do this. What is comfortable and productive to me may not be for you [or the team]. I would like your input into how we can do this best.

What barriers could hinder our success?

How can I help in removing barriers or obtaining resources?

What additional resources may be necessary?

What additional organizational support is necessary for success?

How can we best accomplish this task?

> *How do you think we can avoid some of the prob-*
> *lems we've experienced in the past?*

The Agreement

Listen to their input, offer yours, and create an agreement that accomplishes your objectives and with which they are comfortable. Negotiate an agreement. Commit to it, and identify how violations will be addressed.

Additional Recommendations

Exercise patience.

Offering input into methodologies is one thing; getting people to engage the process is quite another. Do not fall into the trap of pulling back and returning to controlling behaviors if people do not engage your efforts immediately. It may take time. Some will embrace it and participate much more quickly than others.

✳ *What gets emphasized, gets repeated.*

Increase the use of positive recognition.

Recognizing achievements and positive outcomes is very important. Whether it is recognition from managers, peers, or customers does not matter. We all thrive on recognition. Micromanagers tend to use recognition sparingly; do it more. Structure your recognition to acknowledge contributions to improvements in methodologies. A more efficient process is as worthy of praise as the achievement of a goal. Give others credit for the ideas they generate.

APPROVAL REQUIREMENTS

Everything does not have to be approved. While approvals are certainly necessary at times, try to limit your approvals to

important milestones in projects or activities,

transitions from one phase to another,

expenditure of dollars above a minimum threshold,

deviations from pre-agreed-on plans,

situations requiring certifications or a specific legal standing,

changes that have broad impact, and

high-risk developments.

Approvals are necessary to ensure quality of performance and compliance with existing policies, procedures, and guidelines. They are not necessary to increase your control or sap the authority of others.

The Communication

There are situations and points in our process where it will be necessary for me or others to approve actions taken or next steps. My goal is to move from preapproval to post-assessment of results as much as possible. I want to reduce or eliminate as many things as we can that hinder our process and cause things to back up.

The Negotiation

What do you see as the major bottlenecks in our process?

What can be done to eliminate or reduce the point that things slow down or back up?

What approvals do you think are unnecessary?

How can we eliminate the need for excessive approvals?

How can I reduce my tendency to be a bottleneck?

How can you take more responsibility for approving the efficiency of our process?

The Agreement

Listen to their input, offer yours, and create an agreement that accomplishes your objectives and with which they are comfortable. Negotiate an agreement. Commit to it, and identify how violations will be addressed.

Additional Recommendations

Evaluate the risk.

If someone made a decision without your approval, what is the worst thing that could happen? If the answer to that question contains death, bleeding, termination, or going out of business, then continue to require approvals.

If the answer is less intense, then consider reducing the demand for approvals. If the risk is minimal or reasonably inconsequential, maybe it is time to give it up.

Clearly define shifts in approval boundaries.

There are three types of approval/decision-making situations that involve you and the people around you:

- *Individual control* You make the decisions; your approval is required.

- *Collaborative* Decisions and approvals are made in concert with you and others.

- *Delegated or assigned* Decisions and approvals are made by others, and you are informed of the results. Action can be taken without any involvement from you.

The parameters of these three levels can change often. As individuals and groups grow in their knowledge and ability, more collaborative or assigned decisions and approvals are appropriate.

It is your responsibility to define the specific approvals and decisions that fall into each category, as well as when there is a change. Continuing to exercise individual control when collaborative or assigned is really appropriate is micromanagement.

Teach decision-making criteria.

You obviously have criteria for determining what to approve and what to disallow. The guides that you use for making decisions can be put into a teachable, trainable model. If others understand the criteria, the necessity of halting progress, seeking you out for approval, and the inherent delays in that process become unnecessary. People will make good decisions and exercise good judgment if they understand the basis for those decisions.

Eliminate necessary approvals for repetitive tasks.

Approvals are sometimes necessary within projects and high profile activities; however, for the repetitive, day-to-day functions, others must be able to structure the activity without approval. When people are doing frequent, repetitive, predictable tasks, it is important to transition from preapproval to postdecision review. If inconsistent decisions are made or actions are taken that would not be approved, use the opportunity to correct future criteria for consistent decision making. The time and efficiency gained will more than compensate for the occasional problem in decision making. For some micromanagers, the thought of moving from preapproval to postreview contributes to nightly bouts of insomnia.

Support professional development.

In many circumstances, an advanced level of expertise is necessary to make decisions and initiate actions without approvals. If so, help support further education or certification for some of the people around you to obtain that level of expertise. It is a win/win. They increase their value, and you increase your personal effectiveness, process improvement, response times, and ability to do other things. Do not be threatened by their development; it enhances you as well.

EXCESSIVE MONITORING AND REPORTING

Monitoring and reporting are necessary functions. When they are used primarily to control, they are disruptive and a hindrance to people's ability to do their jobs. Identifying a happy medium meets everyone's needs.

The Communication

I do not want to be checking up on you. You know what to do and how to do it. Yet, I do need to be kept apprised of where we stand on projects and activities. I have to pass that information along to others, and I want to gather it in a way that doesn't interfere with your work.

The Negotiation

What is the best way for me to be up to speed on your work without you feeling smothered?

How can I get additional information from you whenever it is necessary without being intrusive?

What ways of keeping me informed don't work for you?

How can you feel comfortable in letting me know I am hovering or monitoring too closely?

How can I let you know when I don't feel you are giving me enough information?

The Agreement

Listen to their input, offer yours, and create an agreement that accomplishes your objectives and with which they are comfortable. Negotiate an agreement. Commit to it, and identify how violations will be addressed.

The Communication

Reporting is a part of organizational life. Some of it we can't change; however, we may be able to reduce some of it. I would like to eliminate any reporting that is unnecessary.

The Negotiation

What reporting requirements do you perceive are unnecessary or redundant?

Is similar information required but in different ways that could be streamlined [be specific]?

How could less reporting allow you to do your job better?

Is there information being required that you think is irrelevant or doesn't give a true indicator of the real situation?

The Agreement
Listen to their input, offer yours, and create an agreement that accomplishes your objectives and with which they are comfortable. Negotiate an agreement. Commit to it, and identify how violations will be addressed.

Additional Recommendations

Major in the critical metrics only.
Do not major in the minors. What are the *few* major indicators, results, statistics, or trends that really matter? Do not monitor everything; it only creates confusion for the people around you.

Extend the monitoring cycle.
Before you inquire what is new, what is changed, or whether any new developments have occurred, you have

to allow enough time for something to have happened. Expand or extend the time between monitoring observations. A watched pot never boils.

Few things are more frustrating than to be asked the same question a second time before you have had enough time to answer the first inquiry. Give people time to actually do something for you to monitor.

Streamline reporting.

Go lean. Reporting is necessary; be sure you focus only on necessary information. One-page executive summary formats for reporting can be very effective. When more information is needed on a particular topic, pursue it in greater depth. Also make sure you ask for information only once. Do not tie up people's productive time with reporting duplications.

Every minute spent in preparing and presenting a report is valuable time that is deducted from someone's efforts in doing his or her job. Ask yourself this compelling question: "Do I really read the reports that people generate?'

Some micromanagers demand reports they don't even read. People have clued in; they know they can talk bad about the micromanager's mama on page 3 of their report, and the micromanager would never even know it!

Eliminate obsolete reporting.

Perhaps your information technology system has rendered some of your reporting requirements unnecessary or obsolete. Are data and information already being captured under a different format that could meet your reporting requirements? If the computer can do it, why disrupt people's productive time to generate the information?

Eliminate "Prove to me you have been busy" reporting.
If you monitor and measure people's meaningful results, it is not necessary to make them prove they have been doing their job. Results speak for themselves.

THE MICROMANAGER'S GUIDE TO EFFECTIVE DELEGATION

Learning to delegate correctly has long-term payoff for micromanagers and the people around them, as well as the organization. The benefits include those listed here:

- *Gains time and availability* Micromanagers are free to pursue other activities when they delegate. They can expose themselves to new areas and increase their responsibilities.

- *Relieves stress/pressure* Micromanagers use the resources available to them to reduce their own stress and pressure. They do not have to do it all.

- *Creates an enhanced motivational climate* Others are motivated when they believe their value is being raised and their skills are being increased. People are motivated when they feel they are being given meaningful work and allowed to perform to their greatest potential. Effective delegation provides the opportunity for personal growth and development.

- *Increases internal efficiency* Tasks and responsibilities can be accomplished in less time with the maximum use of resources. Workload discrepancies can be equalized with individual and organizational strengths maximized.

- *Enhances bottom-line effectiveness* Micromanagers and the people around them achieve more, raise their visibility, and become more productive. Everybody looks better!

To avoid falling into the micromanager's trap of dysfunctional delegation, consider the following steps:

1. *Assess your overall objective.* What do you want to accomplish by delegating more effectively? Do you want to:

   Increase your available time by having others accomplish more of the things that do not have to be your sole responsibility?

   Alleviate deadline and stress pressures?

   Create an increased motivational climate by helping others learn additional skills and raise their value?

   Distribute the workload more evenly and fairly?

2. *Determine which tasks and responsibilities are candidates for delegation.* Consider the following:

   Are there one-time tasks that can be assigned to others?

Are there repetitive tasks that command a constant investment of time that could be shifted to others? (This is where you benefit most from effective delegation.)

Are there pieces of projects or tasks that you currently do that could be given to the person who is primarily responsible for the outcome?

Are there tasks and responsibilities that cannot be delegated due to their critical importance or confidentiality? (If this is valid, do *not* delegate them.)

Are there tasks and responsibilities that do not demand 100% perfection or the level of quality that you provide? It has been said that 90% of the time, 90% is good enough. Are there others who could provide that 90% quality 90% of the time?

3. *Determine a delegation strategy.* There are opportunities for 360-degree delegation. Can you

Delegate up?

Rebound or give back tasks that have been delegated to you?

Delegate horizontally to peers or others at your level within the organization?

Delegate down to those who report to you?

Delegate out (contracting or external service provider)?

4. *Before you delegate, set a clear objective.*

What is the specific task to be delegated?

Why is it important?

When must it be completed?

What criteria will be used to judge success?

What do you expect the successful completion to look like?

5. *Assign the project or task.*

   Communicate expectations.

   Emphasize completion dates and timelines.

   Be flexible on methodologies or *how* the task is to be completed.

6. *Provide necessary training, information, and guidance.* If the delegatee is not trained or provided with the necessary information, success will be based primarily on luck, not on skill or ability. The chances of being lucky, while they do occur, are relatively slim. If you are not going to train the individual, provide all of the necessary information, or be available to him or her for help if necessary, do not bother to delegate.

7. *Clearly communicate the level of authority assigned.* As we have discussed, no authority, no delegation. Communicate to delegatees the limitations of the authority they do and do not have. It is also important to communicate this delegated authority to others. If delegatees are going to be seeking information that they ordinarily would not have access to, the holder of that information must be aware of the authority that has been bestowed. If delegatees are

going to be acting in your name, everyone must know that they have been empowered by you.

8. *Identify check-in milestones.* Determine the intervals that are appropriate for monitoring and reporting progress. The task dictates the frequency; exercise caution to ensure the monitoring and reporting do not become too frequent and burdensome (see chapter 6).

9. *Identify availability and resources.* Clarify how the delegatee will have access to you or others who may be critical to the task or process. This is of primary importance. Should problems occur (and they will), delegates need to know where to go for help.

10. *Celebrate success.* Do not take success with delegated responsibilities for granted. When others have effectively completed delegated tasks, provide the proper feedback and make others appropriately aware of the success of the individual. When people receive recognition and positive visibility, they want to do more.

PART IV
Managing a
Micromanager

*Changing the behavior
of others*

11

■ ■ ■

When You Manage
a Micromanager
Directly Impacting the
Behavior of Others

E xecutives, managers, HR professionals, and leadership coaches are frequently confronted with the challenge of "fixing" others' micromanagement behaviors. It may be the behavior of a manager that reports to them directly or a staff person who is interfering with and disrupting his or her peers. Initiating changes in the behavior of others may present itself as a normal part of an employee appraisal process, giving you time to impact behaviors over an extended period of time, or you may be faced with an urgent intervention situation. Regardless of the time or urgency involved, it is never an easy task to confront people about their behavior. Getting someone to acknowledge personal responsibility and commit to meaningful behavior change will challenge all of your talents.

The primary step in any attempt to change the behaviors of a micromanager is to have the person ask him or herself a series of compelling questions. Even though the micromanager may not like the answers, it is the first place to start.

Am I modeling the behavior myself that I am being critical of in them?

Is this type of behavior ingrained in our organizational culture?

Have I unintentionally taught them to micromanage?

Have I trained them to do it differently?

The candid answers to these questions will help structure your strategy for correcting these behaviors in others.

As you know, micromanagement behavior can be a part of an organization's culture. Many people's behaviors are a mirror image of the people to whom they report. If, in fact, they are mimicking your behavior, there is a great opportunity to dedicate yourself to working with them to change your micromanagement behaviors as well.

CREATING AWARENESS

The first step in any behavior change is awareness. The optimum situation is when an individual develops their own self-awareness. Self-discovery and an intrinsic commitment to change are powerful transformational experiences. Chances are great that the micromanager you are dealing with has not made the journey of self-discovery. You are probably going to have to deliver the awareness message.

For some, this message will be a profound eye-opening event; for others, it will be an intense provocation. You cannot control their reaction; you can only control the structure and delivery of your awareness message.

Perhaps you have witnessed the behaviors yourself and feel compelled to intercede, or other individuals have come to you with comments and complaints concerning the micromanager. Either way, you are aware of the behavior while the micromanager probably is not.

The challenge is creating awareness without unleashing a negative, defensive reaction. Micromanagers are not going to want the input. They will probably defend their behavior, rationalize its appropriateness, and most likely perceive that you and others are being unfair in your assessment. Confronting behaviors is never easy. Some suggestions for raising awareness and minimizing the negative reaction are described in the following sections.

Personal Observations

If you confront the micromanager with your personal observations, it is important to do it with an assertive, not aggressive, style. Do *not* use statements such as these:

> *I saw* you *do this.*
>
> You *do this consistently.*
>
> *When* you *do this, it has a negative impact on others.*

Merely using the word *you* will intensify defensiveness tenfold. Here are some alternatives:

Here's what I witnessed.

I'm aware that this has occurred.

I sense there is a trend of controlling behavior.

In sum, frame the discussion to be about your observations, not about something they did. Eliminate any and all *you* statements.

Input from Others

When you confront the micromanager based on input from others, it is important to have as much information as possible. You cannot allege "unnamed sources." The micromanager will insist on wanting to know who said what. If you do not tell the micromanager, he or she will confront the likely suspects, and chances are great that the likely suspects will deny whatever it is that they told you. The micromanager will then come back to you with some measure of indignation, implying that you are not being accurate or you have made up the allegations.

Avoid this trap. The micromanager will win every time. If individuals are willing to be identified, then it is appropriate to facilitate a three-way conversation to address the issues. Many times, however, individuals want the safety of anonymity. If so, you must develop corroboration of their statements or develop your own information. Before you confront the micromanager, investigate thoroughly. Many claims of micromanagement are unfounded and may actually result from the pursuit of personal agendas.

How can you develop information?

- *Develop a 360-degree feedback tool.* From the various assessments that have appeared in chapters 1 through 6, you can easily develop an anonymous evaluation tool and give it to the people who work most closely with the micromanager. Involve as many people as possible and then compile the results and present them to the micromanager. Such tools are based in anonymity, and you must ensure that comments and assessments cannot be attributed to individuals.

- *Facilitate a group.* You can also meet with individuals or specific groups to solicit feedback, which you will then share with the micromanager. There is a thin line between appearing investigatory and gathering information as part of an evaluation process. Stress your role of evaluation. The micromanager will soon become aware that you are gathering information. You may choose to lessen the threat by evaluating others simultaneously without appearing to target the micromanager.

  Once again, it is important to protect the sources and be careful not to divulge anything that could be attributed to a specific individual. Because of the risk, do not take word-for-word notes on the comments that are made. People can be identified by common terms and phrases they use. Paraphrase, in your own words, the comments that you have heard from others.

- *Address group confrontation.* This approach usually occurs when the need to correct the behavior is extremely urgent or it has gone on so long that a group revolt is imminent. While these situations are rare, they do happen. Micromanagement is seldom a singular event; it is a trend of repeated behavior over a period of time.

  When "micromanagement revolts" do occur, they are often in response to individuals or groups having been criticized for something the micromanager has created. The result is an intense, defensive reaction against perceived unfair treatment.

  If you are going to have a confrontation with the micromanager, it is important to facilitate it properly. The communication must be respectful, nonpersonal, and nonthreatening.

The Perceptions of Others

This is probably the most valuable tool for confronting and raising the micromanager's awareness. Implementing others' perceptions effectively makes the criticism more palatable and gives the micromanager less to defend.

When confronted concerning their behavior, micromanagers are going to be predictably defensive. They will deny whatever they are being accused of and will justify, excuse, and rationalize their behavior. They will perceive you to be wrong because you think they are wrong. You will quickly become wrapped around the axle of "he said/she said" or "you did/no, I didn't."

An approach with a greater chance of success (although never totally 100% guaranteed) is to discuss not their behavior but the "perceptions" that others have of them. It is not about what they are doing; it is about what others *perceive* they are doing. It is not about them fixing their behavior; it is about them trying to impact the *perceptions* of others. This approach makes awareness less threatening and easier to acknowledge, and it puts correction in a totally different light. They do not have to fix themselves; they have to do things differently to fix the *perceptions* of others. Your message is "It would be to your advantage to do things differently to enhance how you are *perceived* by others." Emphasize that one of the key success factors in life is being aware of and having influence over how we are perceived by others. If they profess not to care about what others think of them, point out the potential negative consequences, such as less influence over others, less help and collaboration, and less career growth.

Identify Potential Negative Career Impact

Help micromanagers understand the possible costs in continuing their behaviors and not addressing the perceptions of others.

Micromanager Raymond
Raymond was very upset that he had been denied a promotion. As a senior project manager with an environmental engineering firm, he controlled the single largest revenue-generating project ($5.5 million annually) with the firm's

largest single client. There had been rumors for months that a full partnership was going to be offered to someone, and Raymond had been considered by himself and his peers to be the obvious choice. He perceived that no one else in the company deserved it more.

When another project manager was given the partnership, Raymond was both shocked and embarrassed. He scheduled a meeting with the president of the firm to discuss his unfair treatment. He was willing to resign over this situation and knew that if he did, the firm would be in real trouble. They would certainly pay a price for doing this to him. They would end up losing their biggest client. No one else in the organization had anywhere near the positive working relationship with the client that he did, and no one else had enough knowledge to manage the project successfully. Raymond was convinced that with the threat of his resignation, the president would have no choice but to create an additional partnership for him. He also armed himself with copies of his last five performance appraisals, which rated him as "exceptional." The only consistent, negative comments, which he perceived as relevantly unimportant, were that he needed to delegate more.

When he asked the president why he was not given a full partnership, the president's response stunned him. "Raymond," he said, "a full partnership in our organization bears with it a requirement to attract increased revenue. Over the past few years, you have not demonstrated that ability. You have limited yourself to one client, and while there have been opportunities to increase our business with that client, you

haven't responded. The revenue has been flat for the past three years. You are an excellent senior project manager, but a partnership demands more than you appear willing to do."
In his defense, Raymond replied, "That's because I have to do it all. There is no one else who can be of any help to me with that client. I can only do so much." The president answered, "Therein lies the problem. Because you have been unwilling to allow anyone else to become involved with this client, we have been limited to only your abilities and skills. Others within the firm, and certainly all of the partners, are able to accomplish much more because they are willing to involve others. They delegate and collaborate effectively. You, on the other hand, severely limit your achievements by not taking appropriate advantage of the resources that are available. No man is an island, but you have certainly tried to become one. You assume that you are the only one who is competent enough to deal with this client. As good as you are, you are not the only one who is capable. We have many competent professionals within our firm."

The president continued: "Another consideration in not expanding your responsibilities to partner was the fact that there is no one else currently in place who can assume the lead role with this client. If we move you up, there is no one to fill the void. This is an error on my part as well. Both you, as an individual, and we, as a firm, have become trapped by your single-handed control of this situation.

"Raymond," the president went on to say, "I realize that you could resign and choose to leave the firm because of being denied a full partnership. As valuable as you are to

this firm and as much as I would hate to see that happen, I am prepared for that possibility. Others and I would become actively involved with this client, and I believe they would remain with us. As a matter of fact, a condition of your continued employment with us is going to be your willingness to involve others and collaborate on some of the important responsibilities. This account will be handled by a collaborative team, hopefully, with you leading it. We have very capable people who can be of help to you if only you will allow it."

The president then pledged to do everything possible to help Raymond earn a future full partnership. However, it was clear that it would depend on Raymond's developing other people to support his current client, along with his ability and willingness to free himself up to develop new business. He would have to prove he could generate the new revenue streams that a partnership required.

What Raymond perceived to be personal strengths (i.e., his ability and control of the client) turned out to be the very things that interfered with his promotion. Trying to make himself indispensable and micromanaging his responsibilities were very costly. His perceptions were very different from those around him. What a very sobering event for Raymond!

Try to Identify Root Causes

The issues driving the micromanager's behavior are rooted somewhere in fear, comfort, and/or confusion. If you are successful in identifying the root cause, it certainly makes correction easier and more achievable. However, the micromanager may be unaware of the issues or unwilling to address them.

In your attempt to get at the root cause, use inquiries such as these:

Help me understand why this management strategy is necessary.

So that I am clear, why does this happen?

What is the reasoning for doing things this way? (Identify specifically what it is the micromanager is doing.)

You will notice that these are assertive statements with no aggressive use of *you*. These are points of discussion, not accusations.

If the micromanager identifies the reasons behind the behavior, discuss them and offer options or alternative strategies that may satisfy issues without resorting to the micromanagement of the people around them.

TARGET YOUR EFFORTS

You cannot fix everything at one time. There is no magic broom that is instantly going to sweep away all of the micromanager's problematic behaviors. Focus on the one or two specific behaviors that appear to be causing the most interference and disruption to the people around them. Identify the most egregious behaviors, and target them for correction. Once you are successful, you can expand your correction attempts to include additional behaviors. If the micromanager perceives a positive result from doing things differently, they will be more willing to consider further behavior adjustments. Behavior change momentum is built through laserlike focus.

Which of the behaviors has the most negative impact?

Attempting to exercise total control over how things are done (methodologies)?

Dominance and control over other people's time?

Unnecessary, excessive approvals?

Excessive monitoring of activities?

Excessive reporting?

Refusing to delegate substantive work?

Chapters 1 through 6 offer a lot of food for thought.

TRAIN THEM TO DO IT DIFFERENTLY

It is not enough to just tell micromanagers what to stop doing or what to start doing differently. If they knew how to do it differently, they would already be doing it! It will be necessary to train and coach them in the new replacement behaviors. It is not enough just to stop the micromanagement behaviors; something must be put in their place. This is where you can have the greatest impact in fixing the micromanagement situation.

Involve Them in Determining How the Behavior Will Be Changed

This is an excellent opportunity to model a strategy of involving others in methodology and giving up control of "how." Do not *tell* micromanagers how to correct the problem; ask them how they think it can be corrected. Let the method and means of correction be their idea.

Here are ten questions to ask the micromanager:

- *"How* can the monitoring activities be done differently to lessen the perception of micromanagement and still provide you timely information?"

- *"How* can other people be more involved in figuring out *how* to accomplish this and lessen the perception that they have no power or influence?"

- *"How* can the people on your team become better prepared to make more decisions and take some of the burden and responsibility off of you?"

- *"How* can you begin to delegate more effectively?"

- *"How* can the number of reports your team members are required to submit be reduced?"

- *"How* can the number of meetings be reduced each week/month?"

- *"How* can you allow others to collaborate more on these types of activities?"

- "Is there a way to give others more input into *how* to do this?"

- *"How* can you give others more control over their own time and activities?"

- *"How* can your expectations be communicated more clearly?"

MONITORING

It is necessary for you to monitor the micromanager's behavior changes and results. Negotiate an agreement that addresses this question: "How will I know the old behavior is being abandoned and the new behavior is in place?" Together, you and the micromanager can identify a mechanism for monitoring and measuring their response.

In intense situations where your intervention demands a very quick cessation of micromanagers' interference and disruption, an interesting paradox may occur. In the short term, *you* may have to micromanage *them*!

Monitoring and measuring may, by necessity, have to be extremely intense for a thirty- to sixty-day period. The micromanager will feel micromanaged! They will undoubtedly accuse you of doing to them what they are being accused of doing to others. Emphasize that you are not doing this to give them a "taste of their own medicine." You are doing it to ensure compliance with their agreement and provide remedy and relief for the people around them. Micromanagement behaviors are consistent and ongoing. They are usually not of short, intense duration. Once their old behavior has been abandoned and new, more acceptable strategies put in place, you can reduce your monitoring and measuring dramatically. However, you cannot reduce your monitoring until you are confident that successful correction has been achieved.

FEEDBACK

Your monitoring must result in ongoing feedback to micromanagers concerning their progress and results. The intensity of the situation determines the frequency of the feedback.

The intention of feedback is to provide information and acknowledgment of how things are progressing. If things are not going well, micromanagers need to be confronted with their lack of compliance or effectiveness. It is also extremely important to acknowledge their success. What gets recognized, gets repeated. If you acknowledge their efforts and success, they will continue to improve. If micromanagers are responding and changing their behavior, yet there is no acknowledgment of their efforts and success, they will quickly revert back to their previous behaviors.

Specific Information

Your feedback to micromanagers must be very specific. You cannot tell them to try harder or to be nicer. They must know what they are doing well, as well as a clear identification of what they are not doing or need to do differently. If you cannot be specific in your feedback, you will not be providing relevant help and support.

Reward Positive Approximations

Provide incremental positive reinforcement for the efforts that micromanagers make. Do not wait until they have successfully obliterated all of their negative behaviors and substituted perfect, corrective behaviors before you acknowledge their efforts. Any movement whatsoever in the direction of reducing their interference and disruption deserves your comment. They will not initially be perfect in trying to reduce, eliminate, or substitute behaviors. While it is important to identify shortcomings or lack of progress, it is equally important to acknowledge less than perfect attempts at correction.

WHEN THE MICROMANAGER IS UNRESPONSIVE

The ultimate control over the change of behavior is in the micromanagers' hands. They determine whether they accept your guidance, make the changes necessary, and learn to do things differently. Not all micromanagers are willing to make that journey. What should you do if the micromanagement persists?

Change is rarely accomplished without consequence. The resistance to change or refusal to develop alternative behaviors must have a consequence. Without consequence, there truly is no reason to change. While there are many potential consequences, two primary examples are as follows:

- *Limit the possible damage created by micromanagers.* Reassign them or restructure their responsibilities to limit their interference and disruption. Reduce the necessity for them to work in collaboration with others. Adjust the approval process so they do not continue to be bottlenecks, and stifle their attempts to create their own indispensability. Others must immediately be cross-trained to become familiar with the micromanager's activities. As with Raymond in this chapter's example of micromanagement, decisive steps must be taken to ensure that micromanagers' continued behavior does not escalate the damage.

- *Remove them from the organization.* Ultimately, micromanagers may have to be released. Just as individuals who are being micromanaged have the option of moving on, the option also exists to invite micromanagers to leave. Regardless of how effective they have been, their continued interference and disruption may not be worth the cost. Removing micromanagers must be done morally, legally, and ethically, and only as a consequence of their refusal to change. Measuring, documenting, and substantiating grounds for removal are usually not difficult because the damage done by micromanagers can be supported by tangible evidence.

12

■ ■ ■

Conclusion

The information contained in this book is only as valuable as the results you can achieve because of reading
it. Any changes you make in your own micromanaging
behaviors or your reaction to the behaviors of others is
entirely up to you. No one else can create your outcomes.

DEVELOPING YOUR "GO FORWARD" STRATEGY

To make the most of your opportunity to change, consider
this strategy:

1. Review your results of the Micromanagement Potential Indicator in chapter 1 and the assessment tools
   at the conclusion of chapters 1 through 6.

2. Identify the three behaviors that you believe are
   most important to change.

3. Review the strategies in chapters 9 and 10 that you
   think will yield your greatest results.

4. Brainstorm your own ideas as to how you can begin to do things differently.

5. Write a behavioral change goal statement for each of the behaviors that includes (each behavior can have more than one goal)

   ■ exactly *what* I am going to do differently;

   ■ *when* I will begin the new behaviors;

   ■ *how* I will communicate my intentions to others;

   ■ the *measurement* that will answer the question "How will I know that I am having a successful impact?"

6. Identify the three most disruptive micromanagement behaviors you experience in others.

   ■ Review the two lists of micromanagement symptoms just before chapter 7.

   ■ Review the strategies at the beginning of chapters 7 and 8 to determine which will be most effective for you to change your reactions to the behaviors of others.

   ■ Brainstorm your own ideas for addressing the impact others' behavior has on you.

   ■ Write a behavioral change goal statement for each of the behaviors that includes (each behavior can have more than one goal)

     exactly *what* am I going to do differently?

when will I begin the new behaviors?

how will I communicate my intentions to others?

the *measurement* that will answer the question "How will I know that I am having a successful impact?"

7. Identify the issues of fear, comfort, and confusion that may be influencing your tendency to micromanage others.

- What are you afraid will happen if you don't micromanage? (Either individuals or the situation?) How can you frame that as an achievable outcome to be achieved, not a negative to be avoided?

- What issues of comfort are contributing to your micromanagement behaviors? What adjustments in your comfort are you willing to make to be less interfering and disruptive to the people around you?

- What are the root causes of any confusion that compels you to micromanage?

- What additional information can you either gain or disseminate that will ease both your confusion and the confusion of the people around you.

I hope you have enjoyed this book and will recommend it to others. Remember: You do not have to be a victim of micromanagement.

APPENDIX

Micromanagement Survey Information

METHODS

The purpose of this exploratory study was to provide insight to the frequency with which micromanagement as defined in this book is experienced by managers and nonmanagers from their managers or team members. The survey was designed to maximize ease of response and to lower time for completion. All items used a yes or no response format. Nonmanagers were asked to respond to thirty-four items about their micromanagement experiences from their managers, peers, or team members. Managers were asked to respond to the same thirty-four items, plus four items about their own past and present micromanagement behaviors.

The sampling frame for the project was managers and nonmanagers from client organizations of the author of this book. These organizations were from the health care industry, colleges and universities, aerospace manufacturing,

238

nonprofit organizations, the telecommunications industry, government, the retail industry, the mining industry, the airline industry, and others. Sample size was estimated at one hundred of each managers and nonmanagers for a total of two hundred respondents. A snowball technique was used to select the sample for this project. Twenty-five managers and twenty-five nonmanagers were asked to complete the questionnaire and to pass it to at least ten other individuals like them—that is, either another manager or nonmanager. Although this sampling method does not allow results to be generalized to the total population of manager and nonmanagers in the United States, it does allow some confidence that the data reflect responses of similar groups of managers and nonmanagers.

Questionnaires were sent in three waves to allow for adjustments to be made during the process and before exhausting all potential respondents. Responses from nonmanagers were low after the first wave of completed questionnaires. So, second- and third-wave participants were specifically asked to involve as many nonmanagers as possible. Completed questionnaires were returned without names to the author by e-mail, fax, or standard mail. Identifiers on questionnaires that were faxed or e-mailed were removed, and all questionnaires were sent to Katherine M. Wilson, Ph.D., an outside, independent consultant, for data entry and analysis. Statistical analyses were limited to descriptive statistics and cross-tabulations using Microsoft Excel spreadsheet software.

RESULTS

A total of 261 questionnaires were returned from February 1 to March 10, 2004; 133 from managers and 128 from non-managers. Respondents represented twenty-five different organizations located in seventeen states throughout the United States. Table A.1 identifies the age distribution of the respondents. The largest proportion of respondents in the manager category was between thirty and thirty-nine years old, while for nonmanagers the largest number was between forty and forty-nine years old. A larger percentage of nonmanagers than managers was between the ages of twenty and twenty-nine years of age. Tables A.2 through A.6 provide the number and percentage of each age group that responded positively to the item, and the number and percentage of the total category (manager or nonmanager) that responded positively to that item. Care must be taken to not overinterpret results for the twenty- to twenty-nine-year-old group of managers and the sixty-plus group for both managers and nonmanagers due to the very small sample size in each of them.

Table A.1. Age of Managers and Nonmanager Respondents

AGE GROUP CATEGORY	20–29 NUMBER (%)	30–39 NUMBER (%)	40–49 NUMBER (%)	50–59 NUMBER (%)	60+ NUMBER (%)	NO RESPONSE AGE NUMBER (%)	TOTAL (%) BY CATEGORY
MANAGERS	6 (5)	38 (29)	53 (40)	31 (23)	4 (3)	1 (1)	133
NONMANAGERS	21 (16)	28 (22)	39 (30)	26 (20)	4 (3)	10 (8)	128

Note: Total percentage may not equal 100 due to rounding.

Table A.2. Respondents Who Either Are Currently Being Micromanaged or Have Been Micromanaged in the Past by Age

AGE GROUP CATEGORY	20–29 NUMBER (%)	30–39 NUMBER (%)	40–49 NUMBER (%)	50–59 NUMBER (%)	60+ NUMBER (%)	NO RESPONSE AGE NUMBER (%)	TOTAL (%) BY CATEGORY
MANAGERS	3 (50%)	32 (84%)	41 (77%)	26 (84%)	4 (100%)	1 (100%)	108 (81%)
NONMANAGERS	17 (81%)	24 (86%)	28 (72%)	20 (77%)	3 (75%)	7 (70%)	99 (77%)

Note: Total percentage may not equal 100 due to rounding.

Table A.3. Respondents Who Changed Positions Because of Micromanagement by Age

AGE GROUP CATEGORY	20–29 NUMBER (%)	30–39 NUMBER (%)	40–49 NUMBER (%)	50–59 NUMBER (%)	60+ NUMBER (%)	NO RESPONSE AGE NUMBER (%)	TOTAL (%) BY CATEGORY
MANAGERS	0	16 (42%)	15 (28%)	10 (32%)	1 (25%)	1 (100%)	42 (32%)
NONMANAGERS	8 (38%)	8 (29%)	15 (38%)	11 (42%)	1 (25%)	3 (30%)	46 (36%)

Note: Total percentage may not equal 100 due to rounding.

Table A.4. Respondents Who Considered Changing Positions Because of Micromanagement by Age

AGE GROUP CATEGORY	20–29 NUMBER (%)	30–39 NUMBER (%)	40–49 NUMBER (%)	50–59 NUMBER (%)	60+ NUMBER (%)	NO RESPONSE AGE NUMBER (%)	TOTAL (%) BY CATEGORY
MANAGERS	2 (50%)	25 (66%)	30 (57%)	21 (68%)	4 (100%)	1 (100%)	83 (62%)
NONMANAGERS	16 (76%)	19 (68%)	26 (67%)	20 (77%)	2 (50%)	5 (50%)	88 (69%)

Note: Total percentage may not equal 100 due to rounding.

Table A.5. Respondents with Their Job Performance Interfered by Micromanagement by Age

AGE GROUP CATEGORY	20–29 NUMBER (%)	30–39 NUMBER (%)	40–49 NUMBER (%)	50–59 NUMBER (%)	60+ NUMBER (%)	NO RESPONSE AGE NUMBER (%)	TOTAL (%) BY CATEGORY
MANAGERS	3 (50%)	31 (82%)	33 (62%)	25 (81%)	4 (100%)	1 (100%)	97 (73%)
NONMANAGERS	17 (81%)	19 (68%)	25 (72%)	20 (77%)	2 (50%)	8 (80%)	91 (71%)

Note: Total percentage may not equal 100 due to rounding.

Table A.6. Respondents Who Have Had Their Morale Negatively Impacted by Micromanagement by Age

AGE GROUP CATEGORY	20–29 NUMBER (%)	30–39 NUMBER (%)	40–49 NUMBER (%)	50–59 NUMBER (%)	60+ NUMBER (%)	NO RESPONSE AGE NUMBER (%)	TOTAL (%) BY CATEGORY
MANAGERS	3 (50%)	32 (84%)	38 (72%)	24 (77%)	1 (25%)	1 (100%)	102 (77%)
NONMANAGERS	19 (90%)	23 (82%)	33 (85%)	23 (88%)	3 (75%)	8 (80%)	109 (85%)

Note: Total percentage may not equal 100 due to rounding.

Index

About the Author

Harry E. Chambers is a performance improvement specialist. He is president of the Atlanta-based training/consulting companies, Trinity Solutions, Inc., and Harry E. Chambers and Associates. His areas of expertise are leadership and management development, as well as effective communication, influencing employee attitudes and morale, and successful conflict resolution. With over thirty years of business experience, his content-rich, nonacademic programs offer real-world solutions to today's workplace challenges.

Harry's clients include United Technologies, Pratt & Whitney, Carrier Corporation, Cingular Wireless, Lawrence Livermore Laboratories, and the Centers for Disease Control and Prevention. He has trained, facilitated, and consulted with Boise State University and the University of Minnesota. He is affiliated with the Sam M. Walton Center for Management and Executive Development at the University of Arkansas. He is the author of five books, including the award-winning *The Bad Attitude Survival Guide: Essential Tools for Managers* (Addison Wesley Longman, 1998); *No Fear Management: Rebuilding Trust, Performance and Commitment in the New American Workplace* (St. Lucie Press/CRC, 1998); *Getting Promoted: Real Strategies for Advancing Your Career* (Perseus Books, 1999); *Effective Communication Skills for Scientific and Technical Professionals*

(Perseus Books, 2000); and *Finding, Hiring and Keeping Peak Performers* (Perseus Books, 2001).

To learn more about Harry's training and consulting programs, visit www.HarryChambers.com and www.Trinitysol.com. Contact Harry directly via phone, (800) 368-1201; fax, (770) 486-0164; or e-mail, harry@harrychambers.com.

Berrett-Koehler Publishers

Berrett-Koehler is an independent publisher of books and other publications at the leading edge of new thinking and innovative practice on work, business, management, leadership, stewardship, career development, human resources, entrepreneurship, and global sustainability.

Since the company's founding in 1992, we have been committed to creating a world that works for all by publishing books that help us to integrate our values with our work and work lives, and to create more humane and effective organizations.

We have chosen to focus on the areas of work, business, and organizations, because these are central elements in many people's lives today. Furthermore, the work world is going through tumultuous changes, from the decline of job security to the rise of new structures for organizing people and work. We believe that change is needed at all levels—individual, organizational, community, and global—and our publications address each of these levels.

To find out about our new books,
special offers,
free excerpts,
and much more,
subscribe to our free monthly eNewsletter at

www.bkconnection.com

Please see next page for other books
from Berrett-Koehler Publishers

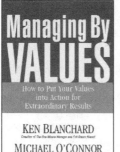

Managing By Values

Ken Blanchard and Michael O'Connor

Based on over 25 years of research and application, *Managing By Values* provides a practical game plan for defining, clarifying, and communicating an organization's values and ensuring that its practices are in line with those values throughout the organization.

Paperback • ISBN 1-57675-274-7
Item #52747 $14.95

Managers As Mentors
Building Partnerships for Learning

Chip R. Bell

Managers As Mentors is a provocative guide to helping associates grow and adapt in today's tumultuous organizations. Chip Bell persuasively shows that today, mentoring means valuing creativity over control, fostering growth by facilitating learning, and helping others get smart, not just get ahead. His hands-on, down-to-earth advice takes the mystery out of effective mentoring, teaching leaders to be the confident coaches integral to learning organizations.

Paperback • ISBN 1-57675-142-2 • Item #51422 $19.95

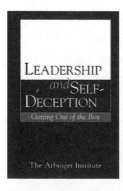

Leadership and Self-Deception
Getting Out of the Box

The Arbinger Institute

Leadership and Self-Deception reveals that there are only two ways for leaders to be: the source of leadership problems or the source of leadership success. The authors examine this surprising truth, identify self-deception as the underlying cause of leadership failure, and show how any leader can overcome self-deception to become a consistent catalyst of success.

Hardcover • 1-57675-094-9 • Item #50949 $22.00
Paperback • 1-57675-174-0 • Item #51740 $14.95

Berrett-Koehler Publishers
PO Box 565, Williston, VT 05495-9900
Call toll-free! **800-929-2929** 7 am-9 pm EST

Or fax your order to 1-802-864-7626
For fastest service order online: **www.bkconnection.com**